Infinite Lives in Music

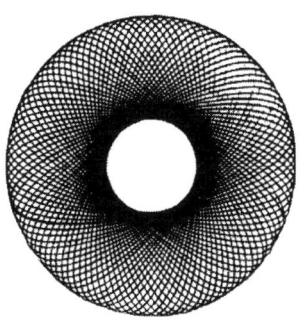

Noah Schwartz

Infinite Span Publishing

Toronto, Canada

For my students and teachers.

Produced & Edited by Cormac McGee.

Copyright © 2020 by Noah Schwartz.

All rights reserved. No part of this publication may be reproduced, distributed or transmitted in any form or by any means, including photocopying, recording, or other electronic or mechanical methods, without the prior written permission of the publisher, except in the case of brief quotations embodied in critical reviews and certain other noncommercial uses permitted by copyright law. For permission requests, write to the publisher, addressed "Attention: Permissions" at the email address below.

Noah Schwartz/ Infinite Span Publishing

Toronto, Ontario, Canada

livesinmusic@infinitespan.com

www.infinitespan.com

Infinite Span: Lives in Music/ Noah Schwartz. —1st ed.

Contents

Introduction: Information Inspiration 1
Section 1: Infinite Strands 6
    Chapter 1: Imperative 7
    Chapter 2: Dissonance 11
    Chapter 3: Evolution 16
Section 2: Music School 36
    Chapter 4: More Than Music 37
    Chapter 5: Failure, The Only Option 43
    Chapter 6: Should I Questions 50
Section 3: Lessons From a Failed Guitarist 57
    Chapter 7: Compose & Curate 58
    Chapter 8: Improvise & Perform 64
    Chapter 9: Authentic Narrative 71
Section 4: Tools as Old as Time 76
    Chapter 10: Metaphysics 77
    Chapter 11: Musical Thinking 85
    Chapter 12: Emergence 90
Bibliography 95

Introduction: Information Inspiration

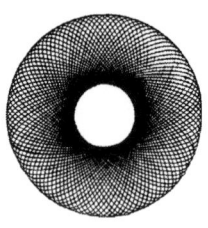

THE BERKLEE PERFORMANCE CENTER SITS AT THE CORNER OF BOYLSTON STREET AND MASSACHUSETTS AVENUE IN BOSTON, JUST A SHORT WALK FROM FENWAY PARK. A home for Berklee College of Music since the 1970s, it brings some of the most talented musicians from around the world to campus. When I was a student I watched countless performances in the theatre, feeling a mix of awe and anxiety. While in the audience, I'd often imagine myself on stage, hoping that one day, if I worked hard enough, it would be me up there playing.

It was in this theatre — during my final semester as a Berklee undergraduate — that I sat waiting for a masterclass from one of the school's most successful alumni: John Mayer. Mayer had been on campus all week as a special guest, giving lessons, performances, and workshops. He had recently finished a summer tour supporting his album *Continuum*, his third straight multi-platinum release, which had won him two Grammys and included his most popular song to date: *Waiting on the World to Change*. Campus was buzzing with his presence, and today all 1,215 seats in the theatre were filled with students eager to listen to him. Yet, I didn't really want to be there.

It was the fall of 2008 and I was struggling through my last weeks of school. Though I was taking some incredible classes — playing guitar synthesizer, studying the history of western music, performing with other talented musicians in the Joni Mitchell ensemble, and challenging myself with advanced harmonic concepts — I wasn't excited for any of them. I felt apathetic. Frustrated. Tired. Burnt out. I was learning so much, but didn't know what to do with any of it.

I had come to Berklee to learn how to be a professional guitarist, but after four years of practicing, performing, and trying, I had learned that it wasn't for me. I felt like I was failing at life, and graduation loomed over me.

Walking into the class, I thought I knew what to expect. I was an angsty, wannabe jazz guitar student — John Mayer was living the rockstar dream. Though he was an incredible guitarist and songwriter, I thought that he would be corny. I wanted to push boundaries with music, he was writing Top 40 hits. I was excited to see him play guitar, but speak about his success? I wasn't so sure.

But Mayer didn't flash his guitar-god status or brag about his ability to write hit songs. Instead, dressed in a black zip up hoodie with one hand shoved in its pocket, he grabbed the microphone and said something that shifted the way I thought about music, success, and life in general: "Right now you're being inundated with information...and your hardest job here is to convert that information into your inspiration, and that's something nobody can tell you how to do."

Referencing the 1974 album *Inspiration Information* by enigmatic guitarist Shuggie Otis, Mayer told us the story of one of his early transformations. During his first semester at Berklee, Mayer was too focused on becoming the best guitarist at the school. He expected himself to stand out and show his teachers and classmates what he was made of. This is the type of goal setting you hear from many motivational speakers: Chase your dreams — no matter how lofty they are — don't give up and you will be rewarded. But as Mayer's focus on this expectation increased, he found it increasingly difficult to connect with anyone on campus. He may have been getting better at guitar, but nobody seemed to care. This made him frustrated, unmotivated, and anxious.

He described a moment from his first holiday break when he was back home in his room, trying to figure out if he had a future in music. Listening to some of his favourite artists — Radiohead,

Ben Folds Five, Erykah Badu — the words "best guitarist" bounced around his head. What did that even mean? Soon, he realized: nothing. None of these artists he was listening to were trying to be "the best", yet he couldn't stop listening to their albums. So what were they trying to be? What was the expectation? On stage in Boston, Mayer described it in one word: "listenable".

In his second semester, Mayer chased a new dream. Being listenable meant expanding his focus at school, developing his songwriting and arranging skills, playing with other musicians, and studying the musical climate of the day — not getting stuck on being the best guitarist. He began to enjoy Berklee, made more friends, and started to feel happier about himself and his path. That semester he wrote and recorded demos for songs that would soon become some of his early hits, leading him to leave school and become the superstar we know today. He credits this to a shift in expectations and context. To be the best guitar player, you have to be better than everyone else. When trying to be listenable, there is no competition. You're either listenable, or you're not. By shifting his expectation from being the best to being listenable, Mayer found something that he was good at.

In that moment sitting in the theatre, it was difficult for me to hear this from someone like John Mayer. He is one of the most famous singer-songwriters of the 21st century. Ironically, by focusing less on guitar, he became one of the best guitarists in the world. Although we both went to the same college, his musical talent is at a level I couldn't reach. But I could learn from his reflections on setting and shifting expectations. I was overloaded with information — from my classes, teachers, books, and peers — and I couldn't put it all together correctly. For years, I focused on becoming the best guitarist possible, but like Mayer, I figured out this wasn't the path to success.

We might have dreams of where we want to be someday, but it's not enough to say we want to be "the best" or a superstar. When Mayer asked himself what being the best meant, he didn't have an answer. Being listenable felt more realistic, he could feel a path forward. Mayer explained that to him success meant reflecting on your strengths, weaknesses, and setting expectations around them. It means learning and growing. There is no single marker of success. If I wasn't going to be a professional player, I needed to figure out what "being listenable" meant for me.

Section 1: Infinite Strands

Chapter 1: Imperative

THIS ISN'T A MANUAL OR "HOW TO" GUIDE FOR MAKING IT IN MUSIC. Rather, it offers a foundation, combining history, philosophy, and analysis to find new ways of learning and knowing. It's about growing as a musical thinker. It's a step towards finding context on a musical journey. It's about lives in music: shaping a life in music and living musically, two parts of a greater whole. A life in music is an external process — it's about engaging with the community, the industry, and finding a place. Living musically is internal — it's soulful, and only you know how it affects and fulfills you.

No one's conception of music is the same. Our lives in music are different. The music we make is different. But we are all building from the same source, because music is imperative.

Regardless of condition, impoverished or privileged; regardless of society, embraced by disease or renaissance; regardless of genre, popular or obscure; music is an integral part of human experience. Natural and familiar from the onset of life, it's the first beats of our heart, our cooing, gurgling, and rattling as babies. It's listening to our favourite songs, playing with friends, seeing it live. Music can be creation, connection, and communication; it's interdisciplinary, logical, and logistical; it's passionate, collaborative, and solitary. The imperative is a call to join with our communities through authentic expression.

As a professor in a faculty of media, communication, and design, I work with young people who are passionate about music. Some play instruments, others make playlists. Some organize concerts, others manage artists. They're writers, photographers, songwriters, filmmakers, DJs, dancers, and producers. Some do things that I don't understand. They all love music. Over time, while the students change, the same question remains and repeats:

What does it take to have a life in music?

I ask this question — to myself, my friends, my teachers, and back to my students — and I suspect you've wondered the same thing too. It's a big question, and the answers are different for each of us. When we ask this, we're often thinking about a few things: "I want to make music", "I want to be happy and successful", and "I want to do something that I'm proud of".

These ideas drive much of my teaching and many of the questions posed in this book show up in my classes. I'm bringing the thoughts, lessons, and advice I've received together with my own experience. Here, we'll explore success and what it means to search for it.

We often say things like, "music is my life", or "music saved my life", or simply, "I love music". These sentiments are sincere, and they might be sufficient if our relationship is exclusively as a passive listener. But if we want to have a life in music, then it's worth exploring deeper, to understand what attracts us to the music we love, not just as art, but also as a lifestyle, identity, and career. This involves questioning the nature of our relationship with the world around us: our families, friends, schools, teachers, jobs, and communities. It means rethinking music, its role in our lives, and adding context and perspective.

Many resources and professional guides give good advice on how to practice, create content, promote it, and move forward. These are vital parts of a musical life, but I believe they are only part of the equation. My experiences have shown me that context is just as important as content.

Context surrounds everything. It's circumstantial and highly nuanced. It informs our decisions, helping us learn and grow. Context is dynamic and always changing. As the balance between art, commerce, and authenticity, it presents differently for everyone. Context helps us make meaning for ourselves, and with it we can recognize patterns, develop intuition, and make choices.

As a teacher, my job is to help you explore your own unique contexts, and that's what I try to do here. Together, we expand our view of music and what it means, placing it in context — historical, philosophical, technological, personal, and cultural. We explore how music as an art and industry got to where it is today, and where it may be going. By doing this, I hope you begin to see music as I do: a universal tool that we use to shape our lives, and a framework for understanding.

As a source of energy and inspiration, music is hope to believe in new ways of being, and courage to challenge established conceptions. It yields universal truths and fundamental mysteries, offering insight into the nature of time, balance, movement, and opposing forces; integral components of rhythm, melody, and harmony; tension and release; consonance and dissonance. Musicians move between these dimensions, searching for the right balance at the right time.

Musical skills can transfer across our endeavors: Just as we consider rhythm, melody, and harmony as pieces of a whole, we can approach our work in art, commerce, and technology as interrelated pieces of an interconnected system. We walk multiple paths, and our passion for music can be a connecting force that weaves through it all.

Building a life in music takes study, practice, struggle, conflict, composition, curation, performance, improvisation, reflection, and authenticity. It begins as an unconscious desire to fulfill our musical imperative, and with the question what does it take to have a life in music?

It's complicated, there's no one "right" answer, and the ones we find may be seemingly in conflict, answers that are simple and straightforward while at the same complex and anxiety-inducing. Often we will find more questions:

What is a life in music?
Does having a musical life mean being a musician?

What is a musician?
Is a musician someone who plays an instrument, or a musical thinker who seeks to learn about the world and their place in it?

What is music?
Is music solely sound, or is it also printed manuscripts and digital files, instruments, venues and other spaces?

Is music thought?
How does music connect us to our communities, our dreams, our work, our world, and shape our cognition and perception of reality?

The definitions evolve through time. To me, a musician is someone who is working and learning with music, regardless of configuration. Whether or not you think of yourself as a musician, it can be helpful to think of your life in terms of music.

It's an infinite span of learning, progression, and possibility, a never-ending journey to make music our lives and to make our lives music. There are many divergent paths, and no singular answers. This is both exciting and anxiety-inducing. So, let's start simply: what's meaningful to us? What's inspirational? It's Music.

Chapter 2: Dissonance

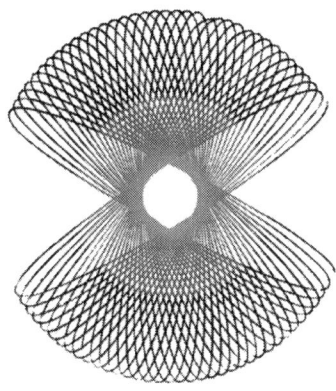

CONSIDER A FAVOURITE PIECE OF MUSIC — IT COULD BE A SONG, SYMPHONY, OR SCORE; ALBUM, ANTHOLOGY, OR ANTHEM; BEAT, RIFF, OR LULLABY. How does it make you feel? What does it make you remember? Why is it special?

The relationships we have with our favourites are personal. The moments we share are intimate, we might feel like we are connecting directly with the artist. These connections are visceral, unfiltered, and authentic, and it's often our desire to experience these feelings that leads us to pursue a life in music.

When we listen to a song on our smartphone, computer, or stereo, we are engaging with something that can be unpacked into many individual pieces. The recording is a piece of art, but it's also a product, which is a part of a larger industry built around providing musical experiences.

Words like "product" and "industry" might bring to mind consumerism, but they are essential considerations for making and sharing music, and finding career opportunities. These concepts are a reality of the music industry, they guide people towards making a living with what they love, and a life in music involves recognizing this context. Processes of creation, distribution, and consumption propel the industry, and each are wide worlds within themselves that offer exciting opportunities.

Music creation might seem familiar — playing an instrument, chopping up a sample, or performing on a stage — but it always involves more than just an artist. Engineers, designers, and manufacturers are all integral to the creative process of writing, producing, and recording. From there, artists share their work with fans through a variety of channels, both in-person and online. Record labels, streaming services, technology companies, publishers, agents, managers, promoters, venues, and marketers all have roles in reaching listeners.

Today, many of these processes are technologically mediated, with creation, consumption, and distribution increasingly occurring on the same device: the personal computer.

Whether it's a phone, laptop or desktop, personal computing has amalgamated many technologies into one tool, transforming the recording studio from a space with large mixing consoles and expensive outboard gear to a simple computer and microphone setup. Artists instantly deliver their music to the most popular streaming services in the world, and with even less effort, we search and listen to almost any song we want.

In his 1964 book *Understanding Media*, preeminent media scholar Marshall McLuhan published his famous phrase: "the medium is the message." With this phrase, McLuhan is explaining that tools and technologies actively shape the content of media. If we look at music, we can clearly see how instruments, manuscripts, or personal computers shape it. Distribution and consumption practices also play a role, with technologies such as vinyl, radio, and streaming influencing style, content, and sound. Music is fully integrated with the technologies of the information age. From MP3 files and laptop computers to streaming and smartphones, we continue to experience the evolving relationship between music and technology.

With this abundance of technology, media, and content, we suffer from an increased scarcity of context. We can take for granted how simple it is to stream a concert or listen to any artist from around the world. But recorded music is very recent in human experience — less than 150 years. As prophetic science fiction author William Gibson pointed out it in his 1998 essay *Dead Man Sings*, if you had a yardstick that represented the total lifetime of the human species, the amount of time you could hear a dead artist singing is thinner than the finest hair. Recorded music may be what we know today, but it represents a relatively new model for music.

When we think about the music business we are often thinking about the business of recorded music, but we intrinsically know there is a much wider world. Recorded music disrupted a centuries-old sheet music publishing industry, which itself rose to disrupt a timeless tradition of live performance. This is a process of context and decontextualization, as music has moved from intangible live performance, to tangible sheet music, to tangible and materialized recorded music products, and back to non-tangible, but through the hardware of computers, fully materialized digital music.

Gibson says that the balance between "nothing being new" and "everything having recently changed" is the driving tension of his work, and this theme also shapes my perspective. Mediums change, messages change, contexts change, but the human musical imperative remains.

Advances in technology have increased the capacity and enhanced the imperative to create and share. Today, there are more unique sounds, styles, genres and audiences than ever before. Forces of commerce and art have merged into a technology-based, borderless culture with an unprecedented amount of valuable creative opportunities for musical people.

Musicians have more options than ever. The solo musician can accompany themselves with multitrack recording, and through the internet, can collaborate across continents and time zones. This has given rise to a new breed of electronic artist, producer, and DJ. In turn, listeners can congregate around their favourite artists and directly connect with them regardless of physical location.

Our own experiences and understanding of music are but a small point on a long timeline and this is important to keep in mind as technology and culture advance at a seemingly unprecedented pace.

It can be difficult or frightening to embrace technological and cultural evolutions. They can leave us with a feeling of cognitive dissonance, which happens when we hold beliefs that seem to be in conflict, like "nothing being new" and "everything having recently changed". This can evoke feelings of confusion and anxiety, but if we think about music, we understand the importance of dissonance, both musical and cognitive. Managing dissonance is a function of harmony, and one of the main tasks of the musician is to introduce dissonance and resolve it through cadence.

Moving from dissonance to consonance — conflict and resolution — and back again is a common theme throughout music history. There are countless historical, artistic, and aesthetic examples, from new instruments like electric guitars in the 1950s or synthesizers in the 1980s, to new distribution mechanisms like radio in the early 1900s or file sharing in the 2000s. These innovations are often initially rejected, but grow to be widely adopted. The blues, which is a foundational harmonic structure for much of popular music, is rooted in a harmonic dissonance, with the use of both major and minor third. With music, everything is relative, but put in the proper framework, things can begin to have more meaning, more consonance. What was once noise is now considered beautiful music — organized sound across time.

On a piano, simultaneously playing any two keys directly beside each other creates a semitone — a minor second — the most dissonant interval. These two notes can feel like they don't belong together. But if we add a few more notes we can create a scale or chord. Alone the two notes of the semitone may clash, but in the new context, surrounded by other notes, they take on new meaning, moving from dissonance towards consonance. The growth of music embodies that movement. It's a story of conflict and moving away from tradition, the established order, into the unknown. What was once dissonant is now consonant, but there will always be encroaching dissonance, there will always be that conflict. We don't have to like it, but we do have to attempt to balance it, because to experience music is to consider the world surrounding it.

Chapter 3: Evolution

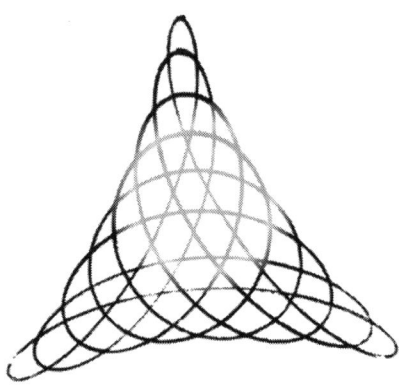

ON THE FIRST DAY OF A NEW SEMESTER, I LIKE TO OPEN MY MUSIC BUSINESS CLASS BY PLAYING A VIDEO. I try to pick something relevant and timely that demonstrates how music can be analyzed from multiple perspectives. I've played Young Thug's self-referential *Wyclef Jean* music video, Rae Sremmurd's enactment of rockstar life in *Black Beatles*, and Cupcakke's body positive and sexually explicit *LGBT*.

In January 2018, I played an older YouTube video called *SUNDAY SCHOOL*. It remixes clips from early episodes of *The Simpsons* and begins with the family walking into church on a Sunday morning. Marge wants Bart to promise he's going to pay attention, but he's not listening, instead he's jamming to a cassette player hidden in his suit jacket. When Marge notices, she becomes furious, snatching the player from Bart and screaming at him. She wants Homer's help in disciplining their son, but as she looks up, he's not with the family. Homer himself is jamming to music back in the car.

He's listening to a track called *Teen Pregnancy*, by the artist Blank Banshee. It opens with fast rolling hi hats, accompanied by lush synthetic chords and a slow melody that sounds like drops of rain. It flips into a steady beat mixing samples of the mid-1980s song *The Message* by Grandmaster Flash as purple-hued images of Bart loop across the screen. This is Simpsonwave, a microgenre of Vaporwave, which is, itself, a microgenre inspired by various kinds of electronic music and corporate mood music. Vaporwave distorts jazz, hip hop, soul, dance, funk, and, of all things, elevator music, to create a new style of mood music for the 2010s internet.

In the original show, Bart is listening to rock. But in this video, the music is replaced with a warped version of what is possibly the most well known example of Vaporwave: *Lisa Frank 420/Modern Computing*, which features a prominent sample of *It's Your Move* by Diana Ross. The song is off the 2011 album *Floral Shoppe* by Macintosh Plus, a pseudonymous electronic musician credited as the early pioneer of the genre.

The aesthetic — or *A E S T H E T I C* as it's often stylized by artists and fans — revolves around the early internet, featuring early web design, 3-D rendered objects, glitch art, and cyberpunk imagery. Vaporwave is a uniquely online genre, blending electronic music and internet memes, and it can offer a gateway into understanding the different ways we can think about music.

We may think of music simply as songs or sounds, but there are wider considerations. There are constructs that guide our musical understanding regardless of genre, geography, or niche, including the laws of physics, properties of sound, and social and cultural context.

Music theory utilizes rhythm, melody, and harmony, and in this context we discuss pitch, timbre, harmonics, and loudness. Acoustics views music as waves moving through time, and in this context we discuss frequency, wavelength, harmonics, and intensity. Culturally, music can be studied in the media, arts, and social sciences as a reflection of society and people during specific periods in history. Through digital media and the internet, computer science is now an integral element of music. In the field of computer science, music can be conceived as software. Software can be inelegantly described as instructions for hardware. In this context we look at input/output, processing, memory, and storage.

Without each of these considerations, a genre like Vaporwave doesn't exist. Musically, it twists traditional rhythmic and harmonic conceptions, purposely looping samples out of sync. Culturally, it mashes popular entertainment, technology, and advertising from the past four decades with nostalgia and surrealism. The rolling high hats in *Teen Pregnancy* are so fast that most musicians couldn't actually play them. And the synthesizer playing the raindrop melody isn't an imitation of a physical instrument, but instead has its own sound that could only be digitally generated.

Vaporwave culture calls back to the early 1990s when personal computers and the internet were first becoming popular. At that time, pioneering entrepreneur and venture capitalist Marc Andreessen was in the midst of developing the world's first widespread web browser with his company: Netscape. The browser's popularity led the company to launch an initial public offering (IPO), which saw its stock more than double in the first day alone. This success landed Andreessen on the cover of *TIME* magazine, in which he sits on a throne barefoot beside the title "The Golden Geeks". The Netscape IPO was unusual because although the company was not profitable, the stock soared on the first day of trading. This set a precedent for many technology companies today, from Spotify to Uber, to prioritize user engagement over profits in the push to go public.

After Netscape was bought by AOL for billions of dollars, Andreessen began to invest his earnings, mainly in software companies. In 2011, he wrote in a now famous essay, "software is eating the world." As a young college graduate, Andreessen understood the transformational nature of software, computing, and the internet for collaboration and social networking. As a venture capitalist, he leverages its potential for business, and has become one of the most successful software investors of all time, backing companies such as Facebook, Skype, Twitter, and others.

Looking at a genre like Vaporwave, we can see how software has shifted the musical landscape. Software has changed everything from creating sounds and playing instruments, to affordably accessing and listening on multiple devices. This transfer of recorded music from physical to digital has lowered barriers to entry for musicians and listeners and moved recorded music from a relatively scarce commodity to an abundant, inexpensive medium.

Today, those of us with a mobile device and an internet connection can listen to almost any song, at any time. This is awesome, and although it may seem obvious, it's a relatively new phenomenon. It's something I couldn't do growing up in the 1990s. When we listen to music on our mobile devices, we're standing on the shoulders of complex and constantly changing musical, technological, and cultural processes.

To understand the issues of music today it can help to consider currents and conflicts from the past. At the same time, we should be cognizant that the history of music is a story of embracing dissonance, pushing against the established order, and questioning authority. From polyphony to piracy, pushing against the status quo moves not only music, but technology and culture forward.

All new developments are met with resistance. It's hard to imagine, but the shift from single melodies (monophony) to more complex harmonies (polyphony) may have been as controversial in 10th century Europe, as file sharing was in the late 1990s when it helped usher music into the digital age.

Studying music history is not just about respect and appreciation, it's about understanding that through evolution, the future will look different than the present. Everything we know can be upended and we see this with the addition of computer science to the foundation of how we create and share.

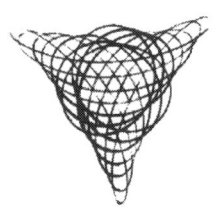

In 2001, Steve Jobs stood in front of a small audience of technology journalists and industry members, and presented what he called Apple's "digital hub strategy". Wearing what would become his trademark outfit, a black turtleneck tucked into a pair of blue jeans, he showed the audience a circle split into four quadrants, each a pillar of the company's strategy: music, photo, video, and DVD. Apple's Mac computers already ran software for these pillars — iTunes, iPhoto, iMovie, and iDVD — but today Jobs was introducing the first physical product from the music quadrant: the iPod.

At a time in which the major record companies were bemoaning digital music and trying to shut down file-sharing services like Napster, Jobs saw an opportunity. Many of the biggest recorded music companies were fighting against the digital age, but Apple, a technology company, was at the forefront of it. Apple worked to not just be at the front of technology, but culture. This quadrant on the screen showed Apple's approach to culture. Photo, video, and media were all important, but Jobs loved music and deeply understood how it connects people.

Two years before Apple launched the iPod, music consumption was thrust into the digital age with the infamous free file sharing service Napster. Throughout the 1990s, the decreasing cost of consumer electronics and increasing availability of broadband internet opened up opportunities to shift how we listened to music. Music as a product was once scarce and deliberately controlled — whether it was limited by the number of pages printed on the press or space on a store's shelves. People had been purchasing digital songs for the past decade to burn CDs or load onto their MP3 players, but with

Napster, these songs were now easy to copy and distribute freely.

Napster allowed users to share their digital song libraries from computer to computer. For the cost of an internet connection, it opened up an entire world of previously unavailable music. Consumers were able to mix and match songs, artists, and genres with ease like never before. Unlike the CD burner or the MP3 player, Napster took off quickly, and in 2000, just one year after its launch, it had 40 million users worldwide.

Major music companies viewed Napster as an illegal threat. They sued the company for copyright infringement and accused its users of piracy. By 2001, Napster was shut down, but hundreds of other sites took its place, and the practice of file-sharing became a central part of digital culture. Apple saw file sharing in a different light, as something to compete with and beat with a better service, not lawsuits. Jobs's theory was: if Apple could create a better user experience than free file sharing applications, then consumers wouldn't mind paying for music.

By making the iTunes music storage and organization jukebox free on Mac and Windows operating systems, and allowing users to connect any brand of MP3 player to the software, Apple was already integrating itself into the core of music listening and consumption experience. So when the company launched the iTunes store in 2003, users flocked to it. The store offered an alternative to file sharing, through which consumers could purchase songs for 99 cents, or full albums for $9.99. With the cost, Apple promised a seamless experience. Gone was the effort needed to dig through file sharing sites to find the specific song you wanted, and the worry that a freely downloaded folder could contain the wrong music, or even a virus. On the iTunes store, you could find a song, purchase it, and have it on your MP3 player in minutes.

In 2006, Apple announced it had sold over 1 billion songs on iTunes. By 2007 another 1 billion songs had been sold on iTunes, and it took only 6 months to sell another billion. By 2011 Apple had sold well over 10 billion songs on iTunes. Digital songs in general held a 30 percent market share and for the first time since the 1990s CDs made up less than 50 percent of the market for all recorded music sold in the United States. Soon, Apple expanded the store to sell and distribute movies, television, podcasts, and more.

While Apple may have owned the largest digital music stores, it still needed creators to fill it. The company signed distribution deals with the major record labels to send their music through iTunes, but at the same time, a new breed of musician was growing. As the cost to share music was falling, so too was the cost to record it.

By the mid 2000s, anyone with a computer and an internet connection could create music and record themselves. Apple's free digital audio workstation, GarageBand, became increasingly popular, along with other competitors such as Ableton Live, FL Studio, and Pro Tools. For a long time, recording music took a special set of skills. You needed to understand the technical hardware, the space, and the instruments. These tools allowed almost anyone to be a producer or engineer, whether in a massive studio or at home on a laptop. Music schools like Berklee began requiring students to purchase Macbook laptops. Graduates left school composing, transcribing, editing and remixing on Apple products.

The "recording industry" today is not what it was for the majority of the 20th century. During this period, recording was invented and reinvented several times, with AM/FM radio, wax, vinyl, tape, and digital.

Digital recording itself has gone from expensive electronic recording consoles to relatively cheap consumer goods. As the popularity of the iTunes store grew, new competitors rose to host songs in their different forms. Free download sites like DatPiff were the source for mixtapes. YouTube became the place to find music videos. Online radio gave users an opportunity to listen nonstop to their favourite genres. Then, in the 2010s, streaming platforms like Spotify started gaining popularity, so much so, that in 2019, Apple split iTunes from an all-in-one store to multiple streaming services, including Apple Music, Apple Podcasts, and Apple TV.

This shift of music creation and distribution has had many ramifications for the connections between creator and audience. Recording was initially used to capture live performance, and its goal was to sound as close to live music as possible. As the technology advanced, recording became an art unto itself, generating a multitude of new forms of musical expression. Soon, live performance began to emulate recordings as they became the listener's primary conception. Many artists today perform with their laptops as a primary instrument.

The music we listen to is often made by artists who we will never see live or are already dead. We couldn't listen to this music without the work of countless engineers, designers, computer scientists, and technicians building and maintaining our global technological infrastructure, including wireless networks, personal computers, and other devices. Unlike Steve Jobs, we will never know most of these faceless people, but they enable our ability to consume, make, and share.

Digital information and interconnected global networks have enabled growth and progress at a faster rate than ever. This is especially the case through personal computing and the internet.

We are increasingly interconnected while disintermediated from each other. This means we can make music with people around the world and access artists more directly than ever before. But the lack of real time physical connection changes the context of the music and the interactions. Today we can choose when, where and how we listen to and engage with our favourite artists.

The abundance of accessible information created a fundamental shift in the supply and demand dynamics in the musical community. The period beginning with Napster in 1999 and ending with widespread streaming adoption in the 2010s is often referred to as a downturn in the music industry, but it was really a downturn for the major record labels who had been the centre of power for decades. These multinational companies actively resisted the shift to digital media and online consumption which allowed new competitors into the landscape who were able to provide faster and cheaper options.

There's more music being created than ever before. Music can be mixed and intermingled in new ways and there is a seemingly infinite amount of new genres and sounds. Some berate this, because it leads to an oversaturation of recorded music, which reduces the ability to reach mainstream appeal or acceptance. But it also allows for what could be considered a return to a culture of live music performance, where artists can build audiences by genre and region, and musical production is less dictated by large recording companies and media conglomerates.

The transfer of recorded music from physical to digital has lowered barriers to entry for musicians and listeners, and moved recorded music from a relatively scarce commodity to an abundant, inexpensive medium. The internet also changed the delivery method for recorded music products, which shifted monetization models for recorded music. As the costs of recording have decreased, so too has the monetary value of that recording. An album used to sell for maybe $10. Today, a stream is worth less than a penny. Recorded music still has great value, but it's not the same 1:1 monetary exchange as it was in the era of physical media, when information and recordings were relatively inaccessible. In the digital age, recorded music can still be a viable source of income for many artists, but it is no longer their primary currency.

Recorded music is one of many currencies artists can use to build strong connections with their fans. But the way it's recorded, produced, and distributed has to be thought of in a wider context that includes performance, digital media, community engagement, and other mediums. Just like Steve Jobs and Apple, we must think of recorded music as one piece of a large puzzle.

FIVE HUNDRED YEARS BEFORE STEVE JOBS UNVEILED THE FIRST IPOD, OTTAVIANO DEL PETRUCCI PRESENTED AN IDEA TO THE VENETIAN GOVERNMENT THAT WOULD CHANGE THE MUSIC INDUSTRY FOREVER: HE WANTED TO MASS PRODUCE SHEET MUSIC. Born into a noble, yet impoverished family in the central-Italian town of Fossombrone in 1466, Petrucci went to school in nearby Urbino, which, under the Duke Federico da Montefeltro, was one of the leading regions of the independent Renaissance in Italy. Montefeltro prioritized art, literature, and beauty in the city, and set the standards of what would constitute a European "gentleman" for centuries.

In 1490, fifty years after Johannes Gutenberg popularized the printing press in Europe, Petrucci travelled north along the coast of the Adriatic Sea, arriving in Venice to study printing techniques. During his training, Petrucci became fascinated with printing sheet music. At the time, music manuscripts were generally handwritten, rare and largely held by the powerful. Printers around Italy had begun using movable type to mass produce simple musical scores, but Petrucci saw a greater opportunity: he wanted to bring sheet music into households everywhere.

After arriving in Venice, he petitioned the government and was awarded an exclusive, 20-year monopoly to print and sell music for voices, organ and lute throughout the Venetian Republic. Three years later Petrucci presented his first printed work: *Harmonice Musices Odhecaton A*, an anthology of 96 polyphonic secular songs from some of the famous composers of the day. For the first time, people could get their hands on some of their favourite songs, instead of just listening to them played live. Before this point, instruments were the primary focus of music technology development. Instruments required musicians to be present. With manuscripts, people could now widely engage with music created by someone they would never meet.

Petrucci pursued this marketing strategy — printing, packaging, and selling compositions of the most famous Italian and foreign musicians. With his anthologies, Petrucci created an early version of the top charts. If the song was popular, he printed it. At the same time, he found another major area of the market: mass producing sacred music for the large institutional audiences of monasteries, schools, church choirs, and others.

Petrucci's arrangements became the first popular, mass produced music products. His manuscripts were accessible, affordable, and practical, and he set standards for printing music in the mass market. Musical ideas could be recorded and shared through writing, mediating the musical experience. With this, the interaction between artist and audience fundamentally changed, reshaping the conception of music. New opportunities arose for intermediaries to create business models around collecting, packaging, and distributing written music.

Like we see with digital music today, sheet music also influenced style, genres and tradition. The Franco-Flemish style, which Petrucci printed en masse, became the dominant musical language of all of Europe. Composers and musicians could influence each other across the continent, and over the next few centuries, sheet music would carry them through the baroque, classical, and romantic movements.

Even as sheet music spread throughout Europe in the 16th and 17th centuries, printing it could still be expensive, reserved for families or institutions who could cover the costs to print and hire musicians to play. For centuries, musicians in the Western world found employment through powerful institutions, including the court, the church, and the aristocracy. Their members would employ musicians to play and compose, and it was a point of pride for the elite when a sponsored musician created, by their bidding, the great works of the day. These institutional players supported musicians to legitimize power. Along with economic or military might, musicians provided an aesthetic value, an intangible power. Music provides emotional connections to institutions and we see this today, spanning from national anthems to religious services, from advertisements to films and television, political campaigns and protests.

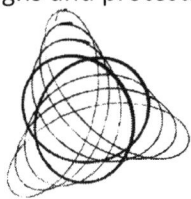

MANY MUSICIANS WHO WE CONSIDER GREAT COMPOSERS OF THE PAST MADE THEIR LIVING EMPLOYED BY POWERFUL INSTITUTIONS, INCLUDING JOHANN SEBASTIAN BACH. Today we credit Bach for laying the foundation of modern theoretical understanding of music, employing four part harmony and a standard system of tuning. While he might be the first person that comes to mind when we think of famous classical musicians, he was not overly celebrated during his life, nor was he rich. He earned his living working for the church, composing and playing for mass and events, as well as teaching students. Bach's existence was not glamorous. Although he was considered a great organist during his time, he was not well recognized for his compositions. Little of his music was printed or circulated in manuscript while he was alive, especially compared to fellow German composers of the era, including George Frideric Handel and Georg Philipp Telemann.

As a child, Bach was surrounded by music. His father was the director of the town musicians, and all his uncles were professional musicians. After his parents died, the 10-year-old Bach went to live with his older brother, a church organist. There he studied under his brother, often copying the music he played down onto paper, a move which got him chastised often, as blank ledger paper was expensive in the town. At 15 years old, Bach was enrolled in the prestigious St. Michael's School in Lüneburg, where he was exposed to a wider range of European culture and musical influences. From St. Michael's, Bach jumped straight into working, first as a chapel in Weimer with menial duties.

Handel took a different path than Bach. At the behest of his father, a distinguished citizen, Handel was educated as a lawyer, developing his musical abilities on the side. Showing much promise, he was invited to Florence by the powerful Medici family, where he gained prestige as a composer. After returning to Germany, Handel worked for George, Elector of Hanover, who would soon become King George I of Great Britain. From there, Handel became one of the most famous musicians in Europe, serving King George until his death, and then his son, George II.

While Bach was toiling in German churches, Handel produced works for two of the biggest events in Europe at the time. The first, *Water Music*, was a moving concert on the River Thames, as a boat carrying 50 musicians serenaded King George I and several aristocrats. Common Londoners jumped in their own boats to follow the concert, to the point where the daily newspaper reported that the entire river had been covered with people. Thirty years later, when King George II wanted music for a celebration of his own, Handel wrote *Music for the Royal Fireworks*. His public rehearsal alone drew over 12,000 fans, causing a three hour traffic jam of carriages on London Bridge. Handel's popularity was so immense that when he died, 3,000 mourners attend his funeral, which was given full state honors, and he was buried in Westminster Abbey.

Although Bach tried to connect on several occasions to meet Handel, the two never met in person. He was much closer with fellow composer Georg Philipp Telemann, who Bach asked to be the Godfather for one of his many children. Telemann was a trained lawyer like Handel — who he was also close friends with — and a self taught musician. He travelled widely, absorbing various musical styles into his own composition. Like Bach,

Telemann spent most of his career working in churches, but was able to rise the ranks in the church hierarchy in a way Bach couldn't. In fact, Bach stepped into one of his most prominent positions as musical director for four churches in Leipzig only because Telemann rejected the role. The city council viewed Bach as a consolation prize, with one member remarking, "Well, if we can't have the best we'll just have to settle for mediocrity."

Bach's music is now considered the gold standard, we celebrate him for changing the sound of music forever and codifying western music theory. Today it is much more common to hear an orchestra play Bach than Handel or Telemann. Yet, in their time, Handel and Telemann were superstars and Bach was "mediocrity." What was the difference?

One thing was the music itself. In the late Baroque period of the 1700s, during the peaks of these three composers, there was a shift in musical aesthetic towards simple textures. Composers who wrote more complex music seemed "old fashioned" and were less popular. Bach's music, which was the grand culmination of this "complex" style, fell victim to the changing tastes that demanded simplicity. As he refused to change his style, fewer people wanted to listen to him, and it wasn't until decades after his death that his genius began to be appreciated.

Handel and Telemann also developed skills beyond musicianship. They were able to negotiate, promote themselves, and build their networks to increase their clients, status, and earnings. They responded to the economic and social systems around them, writing music that kept them relevant and exciting in the era. Bach's single minded focus on his own style hurt his career, and he struggled to support himself and his large family. He faced numerous rejections from churches and city councils throughout his life, yet the same groups tripped over themselves to hire Handel and Telemann.

What Bach, Handel, and Telemann show us is that our communities need art, but they don't need any one particular individual artist. There is no "inevitable" success, no matter how skilled a musician is. These sentiments are almost certain for any musician starting their career but the lines can blur in our minds when we think of the most successful, celebrated, and transcendent artists. However the truth is never so clear.

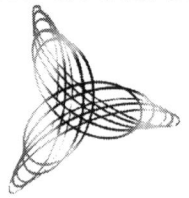

AS EUROPEAN SOUNDS AND METHODS SPREAD THROUGH THE AMERICAS, THEY BEGAN TO MIX WITH NEW STYLES OF MUSIC, PREDOMINANTLY THOSE OF THE AFRICAN DIASPORA. From the 16th to 19th centuries, Africans were transported to new lands as slaves, forced to work hard labour on plantations, in mines, and as domestic servants.

While these slaves were sent throughout Europe, the Caribbean, and Asia, the predominant number landed in the Americas. Through these cruel and inhuman conditions, new musical trends began to emerge, blending African traditions with European, Latin, and Asian influences. In the United States, the influence of African music merged with European styles and transformed into striking new sounds simultaneously filled with hope, humor, and defiance. These rhythms, harmonies, and structures grew into genres including gospel and blues, which further transformed music theory and composition. These sounds further developed into jazz, rock and hip hop, which would embody the black experience in America.

The evolution of race and social justice in the United States is exemplified through the history of black music. Through the 1900s, radio airplay and *Billboard* magazine charts came to define popular music genres of the day. For much of the century, popular black artists were featured on their own charts — first called "Race Records" and later, "Rhythm and Blues", which served as a catch-all genre for music that was played by black musicians and marketed to black audiences. As the number of black artists increased, and the types of music they were making diversified, labels began promoting across audiences. Soon, black music entered the mainstream.

As influential philosopher and social critic Cornel West describes in his essay, *On Afro-American Music: From Bebop to Rap*, it came to define popular music in America. If you look at any Top 10 chart today, you will quickly see the presence of black singers, songwriters, producers, and culture. This influence is part of a complex cultural, technological, and economic reality.

Culturally, black music is rooted in spiritual transcendence and political opposition — a countercultural expression of speaking truth to power. It inspires and is informed by protest, defiance in the face of brutality, cruelty, and a struggle against systemic injustices. It is captivating and provocative for those critical of the status quo, and often serves as a rallying cry for young people struggling to change their realities.

Technologically, the rise of black music coincided with an era of unprecedented innovation, particularly in mass media and communications, which spread music and culture faster and farther than ever before. Before Napster, iTunes, and streaming, there was vinyl, cassettes, CDs, radio, and television. These modes of distribution allowed consumers to not only listen, but watch and learn about artists in new ways. Album covers and liner notes told stories of inspiration, process, and purpose. Music videos and press photos showcased an artist's style. Interviews on radio and printed in magazines offered access to their lives. With more ways to connect to their audiences, musicians grew into celebrities, publicly adored and scrutinized. As the barriers to recording and distribution lowered, more people jumped in to share their musical creativity. The influence of the African diaspora extends through these innovations.

Many of the early pioneers of black music have been lost in time, their names forgotten. Many were purposely pushed to the side by white artists and executives. In the 1800s, minstrelsy grew in popularity as a performance across America, in which white performers would don blackface and depict dimwitted, happy-go-lucky versions of black people. Music and dance were at the centre of these minstrel shows, as performers adopted popular black songs for a new, white audience.

In 1917, the white Dixieland Jass Band recorded the first jazz record, and with it, laid their claim to inventing the genre. Though black jazz musicians were playing in clubs around the country long before the Dixieland Jass Band, their live performances didn't have the reach of a recording, which became many listeners' first experience with jazz.

In the 1950s bluesman Arthur Crudup composed and recorded songs that were made into hits by Elvis Presley, including *That's All Right*, often considered the first rock song. In similar fashion in the 1960s, the British Invasion took America by storm playing blues and rock. Led Zeppelin famously reached a legal settlement with legendary songwriter Willie Dixon for copying parts of his work in their songs, including the hit, *Whole Lotta Love*.

Other black voices were lost due to the inaccessibility of technology during their time. In the 1940s, jazz legend Charlie Parker was developing bebop, a style that grew out of swing music with fast tempos, improvisation, and constantly changing keys. It started as an underground sound in New York clubs, as young musicians like Parker, Dizzy Gillespie, and Thelonious Monk pushed the boundaries of jazz. Though it would grow into a popular style, many of these early transformations went unrecorded. In the early 1940s, with World War II and an American Federation of Musicians strike, the costs of recording in the United States rose dramatically. Charlie Parker literally could not access recording equipment because, along with other social factors, it was prohibitively expensive. Parker grew up in poverty, and his career was riddled with drug addiction. Today, he could have a home recording set up with a laptop and microphone. But at the time, accessing a studio was not an option. Revolutionary artists like Parker have drifted into obscurity with their performances, known to few listeners today beyond avid jazz fans. But still, their influence is felt, through the music and artists they inspired. Musicians like Miles Davis.

At the same time that bebop was growing in popularity, Miles Davis was studying at New York's Juilliard School (then called the Institute of Musical Arts) — one of the world's leading classical music conservatories. But he was more focused on hanging in jazz clubs, trying to meet his hero: Charlie Parker. At 19, Davis began jamming with Parker and a host of other jazz musicians around Harlem. The young Davis would learn from them, not only about performing, but about longevity. While Parker died at 35, taking much of his genius with him, Davis extended his career across six decades, becoming emblematic of the journey of black music in the United States: relentlessly pushing forward, never static, always on the edge of consonance and dissonance.

Davis not only survived, but thrived as the industry changed around him from the 1940s to his death in 1991. In 1957, he ushered in a new era of cool jazz. Two years later, he released *Kind of Blue*, which became one of the best selling jazz albums of all time. A decade later came *Bitches Brew*: a revolutionary fusion album, progenitor to jazz rock, and major influence on rock and funk musicians to this day. His last studio album, *Doo-Bop*, transitioned into hip hop with Easy Mo Bee, who would go on to produce tracks on The Notorious B.I.G.'s *Ready to Die*. Davis constantly reinvented himself and his sounds, from bebop and hard bop, modal jazz, fusion, and electric. Throughout the 1980s, he experimented with the synthesizers and styles that became the base for genres like Vaporwave.

Davis studied and played with the legends of his time, and as he grew older, he was inspired by the day's popular players, including Jimi Hendrix, James Brown, and Sly and the Family Stone. He also worked with, mentored, and learned from younger jazz musicians as conduits to understanding cultural and technical progressions. Many of these players went on to become legends in their own right, including Herbie Hancock, Wayne Shorter, and John McLaughlin.

Davis embraced technology's power and role in music. He also understood the role of culture and race. The son of a dentist and musician, Davis was well supported and educated as a child, unlike Parker, who fought to just survive as a young man. Influenced by his parents and teachers, he developed a nuanced view of the world. He understood how musical talents like his had been exploited, and was deeply aware of the dynamics between races in America.

Even as one of the most successful artists in the country, Davis was targeted by police, pulled over for driving his own car, or beat up while smoking outside a club where he was playing. He couldn't avoid the complicated reality of being black in America, and served as a role model for younger musicians walking the path.

Through the printing press and the iPod, the church and African Diaspora — music has existed at the forefront of culture and technology, as one of the first forms of art to be redefined by waves of technological and cultural change. As new genres, attitudes, and innovations build upon each other, the conflicts and harmonies of musical progress develop.

Music is growing and pushing against traditions and standards — from economic and social, to harmonic and rhythmic. Whether it's file sharing vs. record labels or sheet music vs. recordings, conflicts are caused by cultural forces and dynamics. They affect musicians and businesses in similar ways, regardless of the time period, as new ways of doing things overtake established systems. We cannot say where we are going, but we do know that the current configurations will not remain.

Individuals like Steve Jobs and Miles Davis inherently understood the evolving systems they operated in — musical, technological, and cultural. As a teacher, the music videos I play in class are entry points for students to explore these complex forces. The content changes each year, but the message remains. To be "successful" or "listenable", we need a comprehensive view of ourselves and the contexts around us. We all learn this lesson at different times in our lives. For me, it took chasing my dream to Berklee College of Music and second-guessing myself when I got there.

Section 2: Music School

Chapter 4: More Than Music

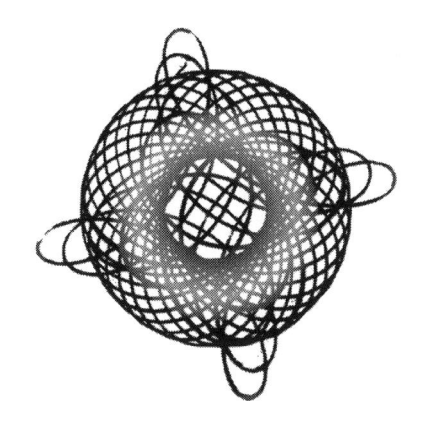

DURING MY FIRST WEEK AT BERKLEE, I SAT IN THE CAFETERIA OF THE SCHOOL'S MAIN BUILDING AT 150 MASSACHUSETTS AVENUE, SURROUNDED BY MY NEW CLASSMATES. Up at the front, a school vice-president was giving a speech, commending us on our skills, drive, and potential. In this room were a select group of students, who had earned scholarships to attend the school.

I remember looking around the room as the speech wore on, gazing at the faces around me, most of them strangers. They looked cool, they seemed confident, I thought they must be some of the best musicians at the school. On the way into the meeting, I had run into a guy I recognized as a talented guitarist, who excitedly told me that it was great we were both here. The vice president said we represented the future of music. My goal of getting to Berklee had been consuming, and I had worked so hard to get here. Yet, in this moment, I wondered if it was a mistake.

As a teenager, I had dreamed of getting to Berklee and becoming a professional guitarist. When we're young, we dream about who we want to be. Often, these dreams can turn into questions. For many young creative individuals, the questions might be:

What does it take to become a professional?

How can I make money and find a career?

How can I be successful?

These questions can be intimidating and we might feel pressured to answer them, for ourselves, our parents, friends, teachers, or other important people. But there is likely no single answer. These questions loom in our minds, and we answer them bit by bit.

My journey started with the guitar. I began playing when I was young. There are pictures of me as a smiling child playing alongside my dad: he's playing a regular sized guitar that he's had since his childhood and I'm next to him strumming on a little ¾ sized one. We still have both guitars.

Growing up, I went to guitar lessons and I have great memories with my first teacher, Pat — learning new songs, rehearsing together and performing at recitals. As a kid, the guitar was a fun activity, but as I entered my teenage years, it became something more.

Like many, high school was a difficult time for me. I wasn't a good student, I didn't connect with many of my teachers, and generally did just enough to get by. I didn't really fit in, and the more I felt out of place, the more I retreated into the guitar. If I wasn't playing my instrument, I was reading about it or listening to my favourite artists, trying to emulate their style.

I started to practice with a new teacher, Rob, who taught me about blues, jazz and rock, and challenged me to improvise with him. Every lesson was a performance, and under his guidance, I excelled.

Being "good at guitar" helped me justify not doing well in school. It made me feel special, and it helped me make friends. It was also fun. Some of my best memories from this time are jamming with my friends and playing shows with them at clubs around Toronto.

One day, flipping through a jazz magazine, I saw an ad for Berklee College of Music. It looked like the coolest place ever. I couldn't believe a university for musicians existed. In that moment, I knew Berklee was where I wanted to be. I didn't feel valued in high school, and I felt Berklee was where I belonged. Getting there would be tough, Berklee has a rigorous application process, which includes grades, a demo recording, and live audition.

As soon as I had Berklee as motivation, my school grades improved dramatically. Rob helped me produce a demo, and eventually I got the call to audition.

In my final year of high school I flew from Toronto to Boston with my parents for the audition. This was the biggest moment of my short career. The Berklee audition is known to be anxiety-inducing. It consists of several musical tests, including solo performance, improvisation, ear training, and sight reading. At the time I believed this was the ultimate test for a musician. Slay the audition and you've booked yourself a one way ticket to musical success. Fail it, and you're going back to your parents' basement for good. For months it was my only focus. I forced myself to practice and perfect a solo guitar arrangement of *Speak No Evil* by Wayne Shorter.

I spent most of the audition day waiting with hundreds of other people, nervously making small talk and rehearsing in my head. Then all of a sudden I was in a room alone with professors staring at me, waiting for me to play. Leading up to this moment, I had practiced for what felt like forever, yet the performance only lasted a few brief minutes. It was a whirlwind. I don't remember much from being in the actual audition room, there wasn't enough time to feel anything, but I do remember walking out of the building, feeling relieved and that I had done my best.

My mom called me at school a few weeks later to tell me that I had been accepted. That feeling was euphoric. I think my ego grew a few sizes that day. When I accepted the offer, it felt like I had just placed my life on a one-way track to my dreams. I was on my way to being a successful guitarist.

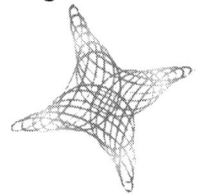

ONCE I ARRIVED AT BERKLEE I WAS SURROUNDED BY THOUSANDS OF OTHER YOUNG MUSICIANS. It was incredible, each day I was meeting people who loved music just as much as me, if not more. Berklee's undergraduate curriculum begins with generalized, foundational music courses, where students hone their writing, ear training, and other skills. At the same time, they're playing in ensembles, taking private lessons, and jamming with both classmates and professors. It's simultaneously exciting and overwhelming.

I loved being on campus — connecting with other musicians from around their world, listening to new genres, styles, and instruments and hearing new stories, questions, and philosophies. The professors were passionate and knowledgeable, and classes were exciting, each felt like a performance as the material was brought to life. I have many fond memories of my classes, even the ones that were difficult, like ear training. The course was taught by Paul, a gifted musician, singer, and arranger, and a warm and supportive teacher. It was clear he cared about each student.

Ear training can feel like a spiritual exercise as you tune your body and mind to hear and sing different pieces of music. Each week was challenging, and I had to work hard to improve. In this class I started to notice differences between me and classmates.

Naturally, although I was friends with many of my classmates, I was also constantly comparing myself to them. While I struggled with ear training, some of my peers had an innate talent with pitch and rhythm. They also seemed to be improving as players faster than me. They could sing better, play better, they looked more confident. In high school I stood out as a musician. At Berklee, I was middling at the best of times. When I looked around the room, I saw a lot of people who were better musicians than me. Way better.

At first I thought I just needed to practice more, but it didn't seem to work. In fact, it made me feel worse. After practicing for hours I would hear one of my classmates playing something infinitely better than what I was working on. My passion for practicing faded because it reminded me how far behind I was, and the students who were way ahead of me seemed like they never wanted to stop.

I felt like an imposter when playing with my classmates, like I had nothing to add to our jam sessions. And worse, I didn't want to. The love I once had for these moments was replaced with anxiety and confusion.

I began to feel that no matter how hard I practiced I would never achieve the excellence I'd envisioned. I wasn't a bad guitarist, but many of the people around me were on another level, a level that I could never reach. I didn't have a special gift that made me stand out. My ambition and hope for becoming a professional guitarist was fading, and it was painful. I was failing as a musician, I felt embarrassed and broken. I was supposed to be a guitarist. It was crushing, I didn't know what to do.

In high school, being "good at guitar" was a big part of my identity. I was a musician who made it to Berklee. I was going to be a successful guitarist. If I failed at Berklee, I wasn't only letting myself down, but also admitting to everyone else that I couldn't do it. This kind of thinking trapped me, and the more I felt like a failure, the more I didn't want to play. And the more I didn't want to play, the more I was a failure. This feeling lasted until I started thinking about the instrument itself. Then things started to change.

Some people describe a transcendent rush when they pick up their instrument. I didn't have that with the guitar. Sure, I enjoyed it, but it wasn't everything for me. I knew I had experienced that transcendent feeling with music, but it didn't only come from the guitar. It came when I was learning about music: the history and styles of each decade and the lives of the people that pushed everything forward.

I realized that I'm as interested in the stories as I am the sounds: blues and jazz as the black experience in America; folk and rock as social revolution; mashups and vaporwave as digital culture. Playing along with recordings, digging through books and the web, learning about the lives of my favourite artists — these experiences are transcendent for me. Exploring music teaches the context around it; politics, culture, technology, aesthetics, plus countless other facets.

I started to realize that being a guitarist was a label I put on myself, it wasn't necessarily what I wanted. Reflecting now, I never felt fully comfortable with that label. I had always questioned my abilities as a guitar player, but also intrinsically knew that I was a musical person. This tension was extremely difficult to resolve because the instrument got me to Berklee and seemed like my whole world.

I love the instrument, but what I love more are the rhythms, harmonies, and melodies, the patterns, tensions, and narratives, the social and cultural connections.

Chapter 5: Failure, The Only Option

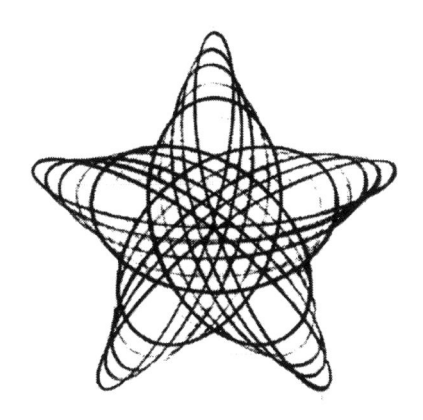

I LOVE THE GUITAR — I'M DRAWN TO IT. As a teenager, the next logical step was to become a guitarist. Yet at Berklee, I felt like I couldn't master my instrument. This greatly frustrated, disappointed, and saddened me. But I loved the connection playing gave me — between myself and other musicians, my teachers, the artists I admired.

I thought I had to be "good at guitar" to achieve my dreams of having a life in music. Many musicians think this way: They believe that they cannot do anything else. Going to Berklee shifted my perspective on what being a guitarist means. The best guitarists I've met are trying to become better musicians, not solely guitarists.

Being a musician does not mean just practicing an instrument, it involves many other important skills. Sadly so many amazing musicians are insecure or unstable because they haven't developed a holistic blend of musical, and often, life skills.

I began to realize that guitar wasn't the only thing, and I had actually developed other skills around my playing and interest in music. My love of reading about my favourite music transferred into research skills. Playing with digital audio workstations helped me understand the foundation of digital recording technology. Downloading and sharing songs helped me develop a love, understanding, and appreciation for software.

Excelling at something is more complicated than forcing 10,000 hours of practice. Practice does not guarantee mastery, and being the best at anything probably isn't enough to be recognized in the community or have a successful career. Taking an all-or-nothing approach can limit our options and potential.

Trying to become a successful guitarist at Berklee, I felt like a fraud, an imposter, and wondered why they accepted me. Watching my classmates practice, they seemed more natural, happier to be spending their hours jamming. The harder I worked, the less I seemed to gain.

Pursuing one skill to the detriment of learning other things is what made me feel fraudulent. This realization forced me to reshape my perspective, question my self-identity, and reevaluate what it means to succeed. I wanted to be an amazing guitar player, but I realized the tangible skill of being a great player wasn't actually an end goal unto itself. It was creativity, learning, and working with other like minded people that was the truest essence of my aspirations.

Guitar was one medium, not the whole of the message. I decided that if I couldn't be a successful guitarist, I would figure out how to use my strengths to live a life with music, the art that I love. From this juncture emerged a life in which I am healthier, more successful and most importantly, happier than I would've been as a struggling guitarist. However, I couldn't have gotten to Berklee without my passion for guitar, or my dream of being a performer. It was trying, and failing, to achieve this dream that helped me find success.

Failure is part of the journey to success. It doesn't mean we don't try, it means we do try, but we must realize that we cannot always succeed. Failure is a teacher and it's important for us to heed its lessons. What was once failure won't always be; when we learn it's constructive, it's the creative process. We can't let failure destroy us, because if we do, we won't try the next thing. We can't achieve excellence if we don't put ourselves out there to find out what we're lacking, where we're strong, and where we can add value.

My love of guitar is part of a greater whole, a necessary step towards realizing my passions. My musical life has not manifested as a guitar player, and this divergence of expectation and departure from my original dream is something I have had to work hard to manage.

Divergence of expectations and unrealizable dreams are issues that I see many creative students struggle with, and these struggles bring forth questions:

Does success only mean realizing our dreams?

If we fail to realize our dreams can we still succeed?

In what context does failure become success?

We need to define these questions for ourselves, and continually redefine them as our perspectives evolve.

Gaining perspective forces us to make choices, and it can seem that from certain points of view all the choices we make are wrong. It can feel like we are being forced to give up on our dreams.

I had to think about what it meant to fail. I needed to figure out my external identity while also shifting my inner self identity in a way that was natural. This dichotomy is the synthesis of our new and old selves, it's the necessary conflict and dissonance that embodies evolution.

"PLAYING OVER CHANGES" IS A TYPE OF JAZZ IMPROVISATION IN WHICH MUSICIANS SOLO OVER A CHANGING KEY. It's challenging and being able to do it signifies an attuned musical ear. Players adapt as chords and scales change around them, and if they don't move with the changes, they're easily exposed as not listening or knowing what's happening.

When playing over changes, we don't have to do anything specific, but we have to do something in response to the players around us, we use their foundation to chart our improvisation. We must pick points of entry, and take the opportunities the other players give us. This approach extends across our lives. Often new opportunities will emerge that don't look like the ones we initially envisioned. But like jazz improvisation, we must be responsive to the situation, and take an entry point, even if it doesn't feel like the perfect one.

When I was struggling at Berklee and realizing that the guitar might not be my future, I had to change my approach. When I accepted that I wasn't going to be the best guitarist, I also had to accept that I needed to develop other skills. I had to open my mind and take advantage of the opportunities around me.

I started enrolling in music business classes, one of which was taught by Sky, who asked to be called "Professor Funk". Sky had an eclectic life in music. At just 16, the legendary soul label Stax Records offered him a job as band leader touring with their group The Temprees. As band leader, it was Sky's job to take care of the administrative and financial sides of the tour, which included making sure the band was paid properly. When he wasn't on the road, Stax paid for him to attend university. Sky would go on to join prominent labels, first CBS Records and later Motown, working with legendary artists like Michael Jackson, Santana,

Herbie Hancock, and others. Sky had seen many sides of music, and shared his experiences through captivating stories.

He explained how record company advances work with a tale of Rick James spending his million-dollar advance on drugs. He described the payola system, as radio DJs took bags of money from record labels in exchange for playing new songs. These stories were meant to engage us, while showing the reality of the business.

Sky also encouraged us to follow our passions and figure out how to make a living with them. He had a winding career, from artist, to band leader, then label manager. As the internet began to boom in the 1990s, he stepped out of music to work in technology, before shifting to teaching at Berklee. Sky had developed an exciting career working with the music he loved. He had worked with and learned from renowned artists, executives, and companies, and passed these lessons onto his students.

He wanted to give us a measure of business savvy, while encouraging us to hold onto, and leverage, our creativity. We could explore many paths and jobs that work with music, and he probably had a good story for all of them. When I thought about being a guitarist, it seemed like there was one route, and if I wasn't good enough, I couldn't make it. With Sky, I started to think about other routes. Classes like his opened up a whole new world of music for me — one that I was eager to explore. Soon, I got a chance to do so through Berklee's Office of Experiential Learning as an intern at an entertainment law firm.

A Berklee graduate, Valerie's law practice focused on musician clients. She was the first person to explicitly show me that a life in music isn't all or nothing. Blending her skills and values, Valerie found a fulfilling career. She was living proof that you can be happy working with music, even if you aren't on stage.

Working with Valerie was a crash course in law, finance, operations and entrepreneurship. It gave me an opportunity to see musicians and their businesses up close — the contracts they had, the dynamics of the business relationships they entered into, and how they made and lost money. It was my own personal version of lawyer Donald Passman's classic book, *All You Need to Know About the Music Business*. I'd found a new teacher that I could identify with: a musician and lawyer working in the changing industry.

Volunteering, job placements, and internships may not always seem glamorous, but can often be incredible opportunities for growth and self-discovery. They can be intimidating, especially as we're trying to figure out who we are and where we're going. These opportunities offer access to new situations, relationships and conversations. We may feel like imposters, and we may actually be faking it at certain points, but these experiences help expand our thinking. When we place ourselves around inspiring people we might feel intimidated, but we are also forced to adapt, become malleable and robust.

Through my time working with Valerie, I gained a mentor and friend who offered advice, guidance and support. At the time, I was learning so many new things from her, that I wondered how I could actually offer her anything. But in my role as a teacher I have come to realize that these relationships can be mutually beneficial.

Through enthusiasm and engagement we can be valuable to our mentors and their organizations. While they pass down information and advice, we offer fresh perspectives and new ways of thinking. At the same time, we can't just expect to walk into an organization and be treated as a trusted employee.

We aren't sure how much we can actually be of service, so we endeavor to listen and have respect for the opportunity to learn. We figure out what we're interested in, strategically choose who we work for, and understand what questions to ask and what we bring to the table. This process can be stressful, and we often intuitively know if the anxiety we are feeling is productive or not.

At Berklee, I was surrounded by incredible guitar players and couldn't keep up, which was heartbreaking. But it wasn't just that my skills weren't up to par, I thought differently than many of these great musicians, something was off. It felt like I was playing the wrong notes as the chords changed around me. Working with Valerie, I felt a lot more comfortable, even though I initially didn't have many skills to offer. Something was intrinsically different, I felt like I fit in. As I adapted my approach, and looked for other opportunities, I found new ways to play.

Chapter 6: Should I Questions

People often ask me if they should go to Berklee, they want to know if it will be worth it. All I can tell them is that it was for me. I intuitively knew I should go, there was no hesitation. But most life choices aren't so clear. We come across various "Should I" questions throughout our lives:

What should I study?

What career should I pursue?

What should I practice?

These questions can be difficult and feel life-altering, and it's natural to be nervous or scared. There are often no clear answers, which can lead us to feel paralyzed, unable to make a choice and move forward. We might ask for help from people around us — friends, family, or teachers. We want their opinions, in hopes that their points of view will make our choices easier. They can give us perspective, but this isn't how "Should I" questions work. It's impossible for someone else to answer them. This is why I can't tell people whether they should go to Berklee or not. It's different for each person. We have to answer these questions ourselves.

While working with Valerie, I started wondering whether I should go to law school. I looked up to Valerie and enjoyed the work I did with her. I felt more natural in her office than I did in many of my guitar lessons and ensembles, and law provided a respectable career path forward. Going to law school became a goal I could identify myself with, similar to my dream of being a guitarist was in high school. It also made me stand out at Berklee. All of a sudden, I wasn't just another guitarist, music law seemed unique and interesting.

But when I thought about applying to law school, I became anxious. Music law is just one sliver of the legal profession, and law school teaches conformity and practice of specific rules, which I was not particularly good at or interested in. The application process itself involves months of studying and testing for specific logic, reasoning, and comprehension skills. Law school as an idea was promising, but when I thought of actually trying it, I struggled with similar negative feelings that had plagued me as a guitarist: I was going to fail again. After graduating from Berklee, I wanted to buy some time. I was hesitant to commit to law school, but what else should I do?

I decided to take a small step, I wasn't ready for law school, but I needed to try something. I applied to a master's program in media studies at Ryerson University in Toronto, my home city. I wasn't sure about Ryerson like I was about Berklee, so I was happily surprised when the program began to greatly expand my worldview. It made me place my music education in larger cultural and technological contexts.

I connected music to Lawrence Lessig's theories on free culture and creative commons and Richard Dawkins' theory of memes, in which he saw cultural transmission as analogous to biological reproduction. I studied history, technology and social justice through a musical lens, reading Plato and Aristotle, Karl Marx, Noam Chomsky, and Cornel West. Studying these influential thinkers and their theories helped me resituate myself not only in music, but the wider world.

I really started to understand the power of shifting context as I studied Marshall McLuhan. Like many students in media programs, I had heard of McLuhan, but didn't know much about him. Reading further into his "medium is the message" theory, I was forced to constantly flip my perspective. Through McLuhan's perspective, images and sounds become disembodied, gaining and losing contexts as their broadcast mediums shift.

For an assignment, I was tasked with creating a digital environment, and chose to do so around his teachings. As a Toronto resident, McLuhan had a large influence in the city, and there are several landmarks connected to him, including the Royal Ontario Museum, Philosopher's Walk at the University of Toronto, and Marshall McLuhan way, which also runs through the campus. I filmed these areas, and layered the videos with clips of him describing his theories and my own original music. I then placed these videos on an interactive map through which you could explore different areas and teachings of McLuhan.

Virtual environments had been important at Berklee, I was thinking about them all the time, but in the context of music — digital audio workstations, file sharing, YouTube and others. With this assignment, the environment became my main focus, and as I shifted music to being just one piece of it, I became more engaged and passionate. In undergrad, my performances felt lukewarm, here it felt like I was on to something. I really felt valued by my teachers and peers, and I had something to contribute.

Researching McLuhan that semester, one of his quotes stuck out to me: "Art is anything you can get away with". Music is a good example of this. Art is subjective, and we may naturally hold our own opinions about what is good and what isn't. As a teenager, I thought jazz improvisation was the highest form of music, and that aspiring to play over changes should be the goal of true musicians. The more I learned about music, the more I realized how limiting this narrow focus can be.

By learning to appreciate different styles, sounds, and artists, we open ourselves up to new opportunities to find what we enjoy, what we're good at, what might make us happy. At Berklee, I learned about music not just as an art but a science. Studying technical methods for songwriting, recording, engineering, and marketing are just as important to music as an artist's style and aesthetic. Viewing music as a science doesn't detract from it as an art, in fact, it can enhance the art. Understanding the systems we work in helps us push them forward, and by examining our interests in multiple ways, we can find new ways to operate in them.

At Ryerson, my thesis supervisor was Steven, a music lawyer who had worked at some of Canada's biggest record labels. Like Valerie, when I looked at Steven, I saw someone successful — someone I could model. So I was surprised the day he asked me why I wanted to go to law school. I couldn't come up with an answer, other than it felt like what I should do, it was a "plan". Steven forced me to contemplate, and I recognized that I wasn't really passionate about law. This got me worried. If I wasn't going to be a music lawyer, what was I going to do? Again, this was anxiety-inducing, but I soon realized I was asking the wrong question. I didn't have to be a guitarist or bust, law school or bust. These are plans we make for ourselves, but they are part of a larger journey.

Sometimes the point isn't whether we're succeeding, but more importantly, what we're learning along the way. At the same time, it's natural to feel bad when things don't work out the way we want, but we shouldn't feel bad to the point of self-destruction. We've learned so much, all we can do is try something else.

Steven helped me take a step back and examine my interests, skills and situation, and with that, another path began to form. I reflected on my musical experiences: guitar, Berklee, law, and my current studies. I liked all these things, but what I really loved were the stories around them — the stories of musicians and their songs, the stories of my teachers, of Steven's students, of the industry and the art — the personal connection these stories facilitate. I wanted to work with music and people who cared deeply about it.

I soon got to do this in a way I hadn't initially anticipated: being a teaching assistant for Steven's music business class. Here were 100 undergraduate students who loved music, and many who wanted to be in the industry. Their major assignment for the course was to create a marketing plan for an emerging artist. The assignment exposed them to the work of promoting an artist beyond making songs, such as building websites and social profiles, pitching press, photo and video shoots, graphic design, and more.

One strategy we continually discussed was the importance of networking. Initially, most students want to meet the top producers, A&Rs, journalists, and agents because they can break the artist quickly. There is a feeling that knowing someone successful means they too will be successful. This was like me when I first arrived at Berklee. I thought being there was my ticket to becoming successful. Instead, Berklee taught me that I needed to start looking laterally around me. It's rare today for an unknown artist to become an overnight superstar thanks to one major connection. While it's important to connect with successful people, it's equally important to network with the ones around you from all disciplines — writers and bloggers, photographers and videographers, DJs and producers, finance and tech professionals, lawyers, community organizers, and many others. Music cuts across industries as an interdisciplinary cultural art, business, and social catalyst.

Success doesn't just happen because we've attended a good music school or met somebody famous, but we can still learn a lot from them. As a teaching assistant, I worked with young people in the early stages of self discovery, similar to myself at Berklee. I enjoyed trying to help students through this stage of their lives, and they responded well to my ideas. Through this process, I began to understand why music meant so much to me: teaching and learning. If music can be a science, then teaching can be an art.

Though I didn't consciously realize it as an undergraduate, what I truly loved about Berklee was the art of teaching and learning. My professors made the content come alive with sounds and stories, they showed us connections between our own journeys and those of other incredible musicians, helped us find our passions and face our struggles. Like music, education involves developing narratives. I've always loved learning, and teaching became a natural extension of that. After completing my Master's, I began to teach more and more. This was never the plan, but when I think about it now, it makes sense. It took time to find my place, and I never really shot for it, but I landed naturally, and it feels right.

Sometimes we can be too focused on our dreams and initial goals, and when we realize we need to shift, we deem ourselves failures. But the dream got us to this new realization. As we move through our lives, we may find values and goals change as we learn new information, meet new people, and tackle new challenges.

My practice as a guitarist made me a better performer, and when I got up in front of a class, students were more receptive and engaged than any musical audience I had played to before. I had to find a new context to feel comfortable.

You have your own "Should I" questions that only you can answer. But what I can tell you is that you should search for people to model yourself after. My heroes and teachers gave me an understanding of music in its multiple forms, reshaping the perspective of what I could do in my own life. You should be open to trying new things. You might find your path starting to look nothing like the dreams that inspired it. This may seem like a failure, but it will help you accept your weaknesses and work to your strengths, because you should put yourself in contexts to thrive.

Section 3: Lessons From a Failed Guitarist

Chapter 7: Compose & Curate

IF YOU ASK ME TODAY, I WILL PROBABLY TELL YOU THAT I'M A TEACHER. Though I never really dreamed of it, I found an instrument that I have been practicing all my life. I work with music, engaging with a community of passionate people. I perform for audiences. For me, teaching is creatively sharing my perspective to contextualize knowledge and experience. I develop my teaching style the same way I practice my sound as a guitarist, but I'm a better teacher.

I try to view what I'm teaching in the context of my students' lives, rather than seeing students solely in the context of the class. I want to help them self-direct their own learning — studying topics and working on projects relevant to their interests and aspirations. I focus less on the information I want to share, and more on how I can help students set themselves up for success. This approach is one that I appreciated as a student, and it's a natural teaching style for me.

In the years before I started teaching — struggling as a guitarist, thinking about applying to law school, moving back to Toronto — I felt like I didn't have a direction. I was anxious, I wanted a plan for my future, but didn't know how to make one. I see many of my students struggling with similar feelings today, as their friends, family members, or teachers ask them: "what are you doing with your life?"

This question can be difficult to answer because it feels like the person asking expects a neatly packaged response, something musicians don't often have or want. The answers are difficult to formulate because we want to do so much, or are scared to be honest, and that's ok. Self identification is hard, but it's necessary. I've learned this throughout my life as a musician and educator. In teaching, I guide my students towards contextualizing this question in their own lives — reducing the pressure of forming a single answer for ones that feel authentic and hopeful.

When I was a teenager, my "guitarist" label provided a comfortable and easily definable sense of self. But it didn't tell the whole story, and it didn't make me unique when I was surrounded by other musicians. Berklee taught me the importance of having multiple layers of self-definition. This didn't mean giving up my label as a guitarist, but adding to it.

As a guitarist I don't just play guitar, I study theory, history, and genre — I'm a musician. As a musician, I form groups, play shows, and promote my work — I'm an entrepreneur. I work with software, hardware, and networking — I'm a technologist. I reflect on society, start conversations, and criticize trends and power — I'm a philosopher. I'm a mentor, a mentee, and constantly learning — I'm a student and teacher.

A musician is a spectrum. Today, I might say entrepreneur, technologist, and philosopher, but these labels can change. A single label doesn't give a full picture, and working in one area often means working in a variety of other spaces, some which we may not consciously recognize. It can be useful to shift focus and explore.

These labels I've placed on myself developed gradually. It took years of experience and introspection as I moved through my teens and twenties, in school, working different jobs, playing music, travelling, and landing in my current roles.

We're constantly introducing and describing ourselves, in school, during an interview, at a party, or elsewhere. In these moments, we develop a personal narrative as a means of self-identification and promotion. As we move forward, labels are added and taken away, we travel multiple paths, rhythmically playing with the consonance and dissonance of our collective and personal experiences, searching for an authentic, engaging, and challenging balance. There's likely no single moment of epiphany. Instead, several strands weave together through time. Many of these lead to dead ends, through which we struggle, learn, and grow.

We have multiple skills, abilities, and interests, and need a story that unites them. We perform narratives, convince others of our worth, and provide value. Each day we're telling stories of who we are — to ourselves, our friends, our colleagues — and to do so, we must compose and curate.

"What are you doing with your life?" Composing and curating our answer starts with our daily activities. It's formed slowly, piece by piece throughout our lives. We arrange our narrative by pursuing experiences: playing music, attending performances, going to school, hanging out with friends, starting businesses. Of course, our lives encompass more than our narratives and the stories we tell others — we are always more than we can present — but we need to present something:

How do we describe ourselves to others?

What feels authentic?

Which stories do we tell?

An authentic personal narrative requires being true to one's self, it's about the things we're naturally attracted to and love to do. It's about what makes us happy, our beliefs and values, and what we think is important. An authentic narrative builds on our strengths, and it understands and considers what the community needs and values. Our narrative is what we externalize, and our experiences are what we've internalized — these are not the same. We don't present ourselves by rhyming off all our life's experiences. We choose strategically.

Many of us, especially artistic and creative types, have sides of ourselves that we choose not to present, and that's ok. But it's important to shape stories around different features of ourselves, because they apply to different situations. Our story changes depending on the audience. This helps us in our careers, and also personally, as reconciling our multiple selves is a difficult task crucial to our wellbeing. Our narrative must be able to grow and adapt, yet stay credible regardless of transformation or modification. It changes with our goals and surroundings.

My value to students is different depending on the class, and I need to adapt to fit the audience. We respond to the situation and tell a story that's interesting, unique, and relevant. This is authentic, it's not bullshitting, it's improvising, it's marketing, and it's growing. The narratives we present evolve to reflect our realities.

The reality of education continues to change dramatically in the information age. During my undergraduate years, we often used the internet to supplement lectures and textbooks. Today, it is the basis for many of my classes — online articles, videos, and social media posts provide accessible examples and discussion points that help students situate themselves in the current industry climate. Further, I see many creative professions combining "doing" and "teaching": authors, podcasters, YouTubers, Ted-talkers, they're all creating unique educational content. Learning is everywhere, not just in a classroom. This has always been true, but is especially relevant today, with untold sources of information available to us in just a few clicks. We never stop being students, learning does not stop with graduation. As a teacher I work to provide students with my testimony of the authentic joy of learning.

Opening up to continuous learning yields opportunities to expand and reshape our narratives. Being musical people, we must be willing to reinvent ourselves as we move forward. Growing is a key part of authenticity, even though it goes against it in a sense.

In the 1960s, The Beatles walked away from touring. At the time, this was controversial. Beatlemania was at its height — they were the biggest touring act of all time, fans screamed so loud at the concerts that the band often couldn't hear themselves play. But with their 1966 album, *Revolver*, the band further embraced new studio technologies, including multitrack recording, pitch control, reversed tapes, and instruments that were outside the traditional four-man live setup and couldn't be translated to the live stage.

The Beatles viewed recording as a musical instrument in itself, and free from the burden of touring, they enabled themselves to explore new techniques. With each consecutive album, they pushed their studio experiments further, blending traditional instrumentation with technology to create their famous psychedelic sound. At the time, many criticized The Beatles' decisions, and viewed their progressions negatively, but now we see them as authentic, natural, and foundational, and look at the band as visionaries and innovators.

This is emblematic of musical evolution, with each progression, whether harmonic, commercial, or cultural, there's conflict. It's tension between tradition and innovation, personally and within the whole industry. When we look at music history, we see a story of pushing against standards and what's considered "normal". Pushing into the jagged, uncertain, and dissonant future. The pioneers of these transformations have to shape their own engaging and relevant stories to convince people that they're worth following. This is similar to how we in our everyday lives promote ourselves.

A narrative helps us advocate for ourselves, and it's important to work on how we present our experiences to our own benefit. Early in our careers, we may focus on aspects that will resonate with others, even if we feel inauthentic doing so. This is sometimes referred to as "imposter syndrome" which relates to feeling like others will expose us as a fraud. This can be part of an internal battle of self-belief and gaining confidence. We aren't really lying, we are testing our narratives. As we do so, we find what feels authentic and what does not. This trial and error process is the only way to find out who we are and find confidence within our communities. It's not about lying, but discovering what feels true and what doesn't.

Sometimes feelings of imposter syndrome can be a good sign. They can indicate that we're challenging and surrounding ourselves with impressive and intelligent people. To be "the smartest person in the room" isn't constructive or interesting. When we place ourselves alongside experienced people, we inspire ourselves and learn. These intimidating environments can make us nervous because we're interested and want to belong, and these situations help us find our strengths and values.

Is this philosophy a rationalization for my failing as a guitarist? Yes, and that's the whole point. Just like being a guitarist was a rationalization of wanting to do something with my life. I needed to put myself in the right context, and not be self defeating. Maybe I'm rationalizing, but I'm also making myself more successful, finding a happier place, providing value, and working with music. I'm not living in my parents' basement, unable to support myself, feeling unfulfilled, bitter, and sad. This process of de- and re-contextualization has helped me guide my students on their journeys, as I have empathy for their experiences, compassion for their struggles, and confidence in their learning. Like music, teaching isn't a one-way information transfer, it's a call and response.

Chapter 8: Improvise & Perform

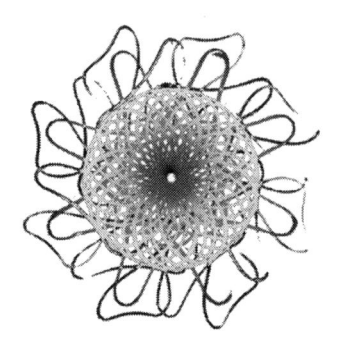

WHEN I VISITED BERKLEE TO AUDITION IN MY FINAL YEAR OF HIGH SCHOOL, I WAS SCARED. I would be playing in front of the school's panel of expert professors — amazing players who would decide if I was worthy to join them. Their sole job at that moment was to judge me. I was nervous that I would make a mistake, or that they wouldn't find value in my music. I wanted to be there so badly, I was scared they would think that I wasn't worthy of Berklee. I was anxious to show what I could do, because there was a chance it wouldn't be good enough.

As an undergraduate, I helped coordinate these auditions, and saw a different side of the operation. It was a system involving dozens of staff, stacks of paperwork, and logistical processes, all moving in sequence towards the goal of getting hundreds of students in and out of the audition rooms as quickly and smoothly as possible. My job was to guide applicants from the waiting room where they sat with each other, to a hallway where they could quietly tune up, into the audition, and back out again. Alone in the hallway, I could feel applicants' nerves. I had empathy for them and could remember what it was like to be their position. This process is intensely personal for many of those auditioning, yet it becomes formulaic for the staff and professors, who have all gone through similar experiences and know that this is just one step on the journey.

In my classroom today, some students can seem as nervous as the Berklee applicants in the audition hallway. I push them to perform in multiple ways — presenting in front of the class, showing their work, asking or answering questions — which can cause fear and anxiety. They can be scared of looking silly, maybe embarrassing themselves — they're scared to be wrong. The classroom can be nerve-wracking, especially when all eyes are on you. We want to prove ourselves to our peers and teachers, and it's natural to be anxious when it's our time to speak. But the classroom is also a place where we can learn to face this fear of judgement. Berklee classes were filled with performances, which have helped me across contexts in my life. In class, we are challenged to advocate for ourselves, because that's what we have to do in life. And that fear of judgement amplifies when we think about our lives and goals for our careers, relationships, and happiness.

As a teacher, I try to help my students uncover why they're feeling scared and lower the barrier for them to face their fears. To start, it can help to reflect on where these feelings are coming from and what we can do about them:

What scares us and why?

How do our fears emanate from our dreams?

What could happen if we face these fears?

Fear can be difficult. But it can also be a good thing. Our fears can often let us know what's most important. Most of the time, we are scared of what we are passionate about. We are all scared of not getting what we want, not reaching a personal goal. At the moment, it can feel better not to try, because then we can't fail. In reality, not trying guarantees that we won't reach our goals.

In the classroom, my goal is to show my students that the more they face these fears and pursue their passions, the more happiness and success they're likely to experience. This concept is intuitively understood, but it can be difficult to put into practice, because these feelings of fear are visceral. Even if you know in your head that you should try, there may be a bad feeling in your gut stopping you. But you have to push past this. You need to show your work, ask a question, perform in whatever context you have.

Practices of performance and improvisation are universal components of communication and culture, and developing the skills for a successful performance are important, whether we want to be at centre stage or not. I learned that I'm a good performer, just not with the guitar.

Performance is how we share and communicate with each other. When we perform, we play, but we also do much more. It simultaneously requires practice, preparation, planning, composition, and curation, plus a willingness to adapt, be spontaneous, and respond to the people and other factors around us. Performance can be how we act in a certain moment, it's how we listen, anticipate, and balance emotions and fears. It's how we carry ourselves and interact with people, how we build our reputation. We can identify any of these aspects in an on-stage performance, but they're just as present in our daily lives.

We're performing anytime we present our ideas to others — from engaging in meetings and collaborative projects to networking and interviewing for our careers. We are always practicing and performing. Performing tests our skills, beliefs, and assumptions. It helps us understand if we're on the right path or the wrong one. If we're not willing to be wrong, we won't have as many opportunities to get it right. The only way to move past this, to learn and grow, is to do what scares us. Present our work, take the input, see what people liked, and what they didn't. Some people perform without much preparation, and they're bad. On the other hand, some focus too much on preparation without engaging the community to test themselves. They don't allow themselves to fail. We can't let fear hinder us.

The best performers can improvise, and they have years of study and practice to lean on when they need to do so. Charlie Parker, one of the greatest and most innovative improvisers of all time, had a philosophy: "learn everything and forget all that shit". Rigorous practice is required for the freedom necessary to explore new possibilities. The best performers are well prepared, but don't let their preparedness and plans hold them back in finding new ways to express themselves in the moment.

The more we know, the more we can forget, and this allows us to improvise and perform what is necessary at any given time. Practice is necessary, but likely won't be sufficient, as many of the challenges we face take forms that we cannot fully prepare for or understand. The best improvisers deeply understand foundational and universal structures, and use them to create new sounds and styles on the fly.

In music theory there are 12 notes and the challenge, and fun, in creation is putting them together in unique ways. Even though there are infinite permutations, there are also infinite similarities. We are building upon and within a structure and foundation. Improvisers can adapt and innovate as they interact with the world around them, but nothing is ever forgotten, it's foundational, it's the shoulders on which we stand.

Facing fears can provide some of the most productive and life altering experiences. I faced a fear at my Berklee audition, where there would be no clearer definition of my competency. The audition tested what I thought was the most valuable skill for a musician, and getting through it showed me I was meant to be a guitarist — ready to be a performer and improviser like Charlie Parker. But Berklee would show me that I needed to expand my vision of performance to include something else: production.

New Berklee students begin on the same general path, segmenting into different majors over time. During my time, the most competitive major was Music Production and Engineering. There are as many Berklee grads working as successful producers, beatmakers, and engineers as there are jazz and rock players. I initially disregarded this major because I thought of myself as a traditional guitarist. Production felt like a different path, for other people who weren't as good musicians. It's obvious to me now that this couldn't be further from the truth.

As I moved through Berklee, I noticed the great performers around me — both students and teachers — were not singularly thinking about performance. They were thinking about pushing themselves and their music out into the world, and getting themselves noticed. They were thinking about production, technology, and personal growth. This was the mid-2000s, in which online culture and early social networking websites emphasized user-generated content, ease of use, and participatory culture.

Myspace was at its peak and YouTube was just starting to take off. Home recording was becoming less expensive and software programs like Ableton and Fruity Loops were becoming increasingly popular. Many of the classmates who I looked up to as performers were focused on improving their production skills to create original music, record songs quickly, and shoot videos to promote themselves online. I realized that being a musician didn't mean choosing performance or production, it meant learning to work with both. Even with my initial Berklee application, which mixed a recording and live audition, this duality was present.

In my final year, I enrolled in a career planning class taught by an older professor named Fred. Fred had the feeling of someone who had seen all sides of music. As a trombone player, he performed alongside Nat King Cole and Louis Armstrong, sat in orchestras across the country, and played in army bands when he was serving in the military. When I met him, Fred had already been at Berklee for decades, teaching a wide range of subjects, from performance to instrument repair. Through his experiences, Fred showed us the importance of shaping our narratives authentically in different contexts, and I began thinking about how I presented myself in these different aspects of my life, in person and online. He reinforced the belief that performance or production are inherently connected, whether we're at school, playing on stage, scoring a film, engineering a recording session, or posting on social media.

For the final assignment in this career planning class, we had to reflect on our time at Berklee and what we hoped to achieve after we graduated. I still have the assignment today; it represents a turning point in my life. I was 20 years old, and though I had struggled with my self-definition at Berklee, I was beginning to break out of my narrow vision of performance. As part of the reflection, I wrote: "At this point I love music as much as I ever have and have been lucky enough to explore vast amounts of this human phenomenon. Now I realize my musical life consists of more activities than just guitar playing. I wish to pursue music related business ventures. As well, I am interested in studying law and writing. I want to be a musician, an author, an entrepreneur, a lawyer, and most of all a human being."

Fred's class was about self definition. Everyone in the classroom was a musician, but for each person, that definition meant something different. Fred showed us that definitions constantly change. He exemplified this through his life, shifting from soldier, to session performer, to teacher. These experiences added up to a greater whole of someone who could show you how to repair your instrument and just as easily as play it. Fred helped us put life in the context of music, something I try to do today in my classes.

If we look at our daily activities, from the anxiety inducing to the mundane, we can understand how musical skills and creative passions help us in situations we might not traditionally consider "music". The research skills we develop by studying our favourite artists, the discipline it takes to practice, the performance, improvisation, and courage needed to immerse ourselves in an unfamiliar scene — our musical experiences are helpful no matter what our careers look like. The lessons we learn have infinite permutations. Today, a musician's ability to produce, perform, and improvise, whether in the boardroom, with a camera, or even in front of a class, is what can set them apart.

Chapter 9: Authentic Narrative

A MUSICIAN MANIPULATES SOUND, RHYTHMICALLY WEAVES MELODY INTO HARMONY, AND USES TECHNOLOGY TO MAKE ART. Musicians express themselves and reflect their environments.

We can analyze music in many ways, each with its own multidimensional worlds of learning. Theoretically, we can describe it rhythmically, melodically, and harmonically. Scientifically we can study music physically, acoustically, and sonically. Socially we can discuss it politically, commercially, and emotionally. Within these worlds, we deeply assess music from diverse perspectives.

We recognize that there are many opportunities, though it's not possible to pursue them all. We can't learn to be musicians, lawyers, recording engineers, and computer scientists at the same time, but trying to be just one is often limiting. These roles all include a variety of skills that must be considered, and lasting success requires a willingness to take on multiple responsibilities, learn lessons from the past and embrace the future. It's no easy task, but it's the balance of a musical life. We can't pursue every goal at once, nor can we have a singular focus.

We can recognize a wider spectrum of opportunity and possibility by accepting that a broad range of skills are necessary, yet likely no single one will be sufficient. This acceptance can expand our imagination and allow us to dream. When we are open to new directions, we're gaining opportunity — not losing.

Trying, failing, and moving is not only necessary, but can be success in itself. Through a process of creation, destruction, and discovery, we begin to understand what feels natural, what we enjoy, what our strengths are, and where we're weak. By considering these dimensions we can start developing a holistic view of our potential.

This process requires reflection. It's important that we take time to study, introspect, and consider what we want. This isn't to just say "I want to make music", but to think about how we actually do this.

When we create and share, we engage with thought and physicality — the processes of expressing ourselves to the world through composing, arranging, producing, mixing, performing, DJing, or any other activity. Music is practically realized, but it never begins fully formed. When we play, we bring emotion into existence. Music begins personally and evolves to embody the technological, political, historical, and economic contexts around it.

We experience this when we listen too. Consider a favourite song. We can study the genre, arrangement, or instrumentation. We can think about how it makes us feel and research its cultural significance, popularity, and what others think. Any one of these facets can give us a view that feels quite consuming, but it's incomplete. Only when we account for multiple dimensions can we develop a fuller picture and gain a meaningful understanding. It can be fun and easy to get sucked into one vision or singular aspect. Almost everyone has some sort of personal conception of what music means and why it's important. We can get stuck, unwilling to consider different perspectives. We can lose the bigger picture.

Saying "I want to make music" is similar to "I want to be rich and successful" or "I want to make hit songs" or "I want to be a rockstar". It may be a starting point, but it's not enough. We must think deeply about skills, needs, and opportunities. We must be aware of what we want, what's valued, and what we're good at. We face dissonance and conflict, constantly learning and reflecting, whether consciously or not. Purposely introspecting can help. By asking ourselves questions, we can work towards a balance.

The questions we can ask are musical, technological, and cultural; they're philosophical, scientific, and social; they're soulful, intimate, and tribal.

Voice. Vibe. Vision:
Who am I? Who do I want to be?
How can I live a musical life? How do I become a (better) musician?

These questions represent a foundation: thoughts and feelings. They emanate from our desire to create and share — the musical imperative that drives passion. They represent the messages behind the music, thought, and essence. These esoteric questions can help us explore internal worlds and bring forth conflicting emotions and desires. Being honest, accepting weaknesses and strengths, and finding confidence are difficult tasks, yet essential emotional processes.

Songs. Sounds. Styles:
Where am I? Where do I want to be?
What does music mean? Where can it take me?

These questions compel us to start looking at external worlds: our relationships, abilities, and instruments. They help us consider how music is realized and the influence of the technology used in its creation and distribution. We take stock of the current situation — where we live and work, who we spend our time with, how we fill our days — and how it makes us feel. We can think about the future and assess what it might take to become better versions of ourselves. This can illuminate gaps in our knowledge and inform our decision making.

Past. Future. Present:
Where's my community? How can I provide value?
What's my role? How can I make something that I'm proud of?

These questions remind us that music does not live in a vacuum and opportunities change as culture and technology shift. Being open-minded and adaptable can help us situate within these many contexts. We may not attain childhood dreams, but we have the power to shape a happy life. A successful musician has an audience, but a musician is truly successful when that audience values their authentic expression.

These sets of questions work in conjunction, influencing each other, and our understanding continuously evolves. They are potential starting points, forcing us to examine our most basic values and dreams, and they open our minds to even more questions. From here, it's up to us to ask the specific questions for our lives. Some will feel simple, others more complicated, and we want to do our best to solve each one. Sometimes we will feel like we've succeeded, but often, especially when starting out, we'll feel like we've failed. Failing is important. It's painful, but critical in order to find our next questions.

As a teenager, my questions included "How can I play like my heroes?" and "What do I need to do to get into Berklee?". At Berklee, they evolved: "Am I a guitarist?", "Do I want to be?", "What else is there to do in music?". As I've grown, the questions have expanded to include more people: "What is learning?", "Am I a teacher? What does that mean?", "How do I give back to my community?".

I feel that I've answered some of these, others linger in my mind. Often, it's not finding the answer that is important, but figuring out what questions to ask, because they guide us to new opportunities, new questions, values, and goals. So, what are your questions? They may be specific: "Where can I play live?" or "How do I improve my production skills?". They may be broader: "How do I make connections in the industry?" or "What makes me musical?". Whatever they are, it's important to ask these questions of yourself, they can guide the steps in your journey.

Our lives can be interpreted as a series of questions and attempted answers. They don't get easier over time, and we often feel lost. We have intuition and logic, we have observation and education, but we don't necessarily have a solid model. We won't have the same questions or answers as we move through life, and we won't know if we're right. What we can do is remember that we are not alone, these struggles are not unusual, and through reflection, we can understand why we made our decisions. It takes courage and strength to manifest new ideas and change our realities. This is true for art and music, but also our lives and careers. We can stay true to ourselves, to learning, and to our passions. We can have faith in music and commit to performing in a broad range of contexts.

Section 4: Tools as Old as Time

Chapter 10: Metaphysics

IF THE QUESTION IS: HOW DO WE HAVE A LIFE IN MUSIC? THE ANSWER IS: WHAT'S MUSIC? This question is difficult because the answer is whatever we make of it. Music isn't singular; it's business, it's culture, it's technology, and we need to figure out what it means to us.

In 1973, Leonard Bernstein held a series of lectures titled *The Unanswered Question*, which he named after a 1908 composition by Charles Ives. In the series, he tackled the notion of embracing ambiguity. He described a "crisis" in music, in which so much dissonance had entered music that it was difficult to discern what was consonant and dissonant. While many viewed this as an issue, Bernstein saw an opportunity: embracing ambiguity shapes new styles, sounds, and genres that move the art forward.

In an earlier work, *The Infinite Variety of Music*, he wrote, "the whole point of musical creation, however, is not to write those notes in scale-wise order only, but to change their order so as to produce melodic meaning". That, he wrote, is the infinite variety of the creative human spirit.

In *The Unanswered Question*, Bernstein spoke about "the interdisciplinary spirit" and declared: "the best way to know a thing is in the context of another discipline". A concept doesn't stand on its own, it's inexorably linked to other thoughts, topics, and subject areas. Bernstein lived this belief. Possibly known best for scoring *West Side Story*, he excelled as a musician, conductor, teacher, television personality, and author, all of which he saw as an extension of music.

We know music is shaped by economic, social, and technological conditions. Intrinsically, we also know it's a link — connecting us to our emotions, to other people, and to the world around us. For a long time, it has also been used as a tool to connect disciplines. Our ancestors used music as a tool to explore philosophy and spirituality. For much of history, it went hand in hand with metaphysics, a branch of philosophy that ponders the nature of being and the nature of the universe.

The ancient Indian civilization, roughly 1750 BCE onwards, viewed the world in terms of energy, and music was a big part of that. The Vedas — the oldest scriptures in Hinduism — include the "Om" symbol — ॐ — a sacred sound described as the cosmic hum or bridge to infinity. The society also explored a metaphysical system called Nāda, which was equally a philosophy, medicine, and physical yoga practice. In it, sound and music play an intermediary role in achieving deeper unity between the inner and outer cosmos.

Over one thousand years later in Ancient Greece, Pythagoras studied music not solely as sound, but as a way of interacting with the cosmos. Musicians weren't just playing music when they picked up an instrument, they were trying to understand the universe. Pythagoras coined "Musica universalis" or "Music of the spheres", through which the celestial bodies could be understood to move in intervals similar to notes on a stringed instrument.

Another thousand years later in Rome, Boethius studied what he called "Musica humana", the harmony of the human body and spirit. Harmony for Boethius was unification, and it's not limited to music. He explored harmony of mathematics, philosophy, and politics. His work influenced the Quadrivium, the Medieval university education, through which arithmetic, geometry, music, and astronomy were viewed as interconnected and inseparable.

Mastery of music is multidimensional, and we have to accept this dimensionality and then decide how to proceed — which paths to follow, what to learn. The only way to do this is to decide what matters to us, because we can't pursue everything at once, but we can't pursue just one dimension either. We cannot just conceive of music as being composed, or performed, or recorded. We intrinsically know it's more than that, it's the connections that matter.

IN 1926, LEGENDARY INVENTOR NIKOLA TESLA DISCUSSED HIS VISION OF A CONNECTED WORLD, STATING THAT WIRELESS COMMUNICATION WOULD ONE DAY TURN THE EARTH INTO A SINGULAR BRAIN. He predicted the ability to communicate through "instruments" that could fit in our pockets. Today, this vision is realized with the internet and smartphones. Communication, knowledge, and media have become more accessible, and music is an integral part of this connected world. We can view the smartphone as the ultimate "instrument" — a device through which we create, share, and collaborate. These technologies intrinsically connect us.

However, the smartphone is not the first all-encompassing tool. The Ancient Greeks had a single-stringed instrument called the monochord. Similar to the smartphone, the monochord was used as a general purpose device, it was viewed as a tool to connect humans and the universe. Music, mathematics, and astronomy were linked through the monochord, and the instrument's individual notes could represent the planets, gods, or parts of the body. It was believed that studying the monochord could yield information relevant in multiple contexts.

Today, the smartphone is a widespread, general purpose technology. It's mobile, connected to the internet, and a point of production, distribution, and consumption. It's an all-encompassing instrument, a gateway to learning and connecting.

Our common experience in the modern digital world is social — we can learn about and join communities, or build our own. We can find identity and strength as we engage with people and ideas from all around the world. We create, share and interact. This social web rose to prominence during my undergraduate years in the mid-2000s, with sites like Myspace, YouTube, and Facebook.

YouTube was particularly important for me and my classmates. Through the 1990s and early 2000s, the only way to watch footage of concerts, lectures, or instructional tutorials was by buying physical copies or trading bootleg versions. Then all of a sudden, many were widely available, thanks to users uploading them to YouTube. The amount of new information was incredible and overwhelming.

Myspace was also an important website for musicians, as it opened up an early form of digital networking. Not only could artists distribute their music, they could also make their press kits, biographies and photos widely accessible for the first time. It became much easier to connect with listeners, concert promoters, or DJs, because a simple Myspace link held all the information. At the time, it seemed like if you didn't have a Myspace page, you were lagging behind. It was a trend you needed to keep up with. But over time, Myspace's popularity declined. As the audience left the website, musicians adapted to using the next big platforms.

We can view our instrument — be it a guitar, synth or set of turntables — as an extension of ourselves, something we can manipulate to sound just right. As a teacher, I try to help my students view all technology in the same way. The smartphone and internet offer rich potentials and affordances for knowledge, art, and collaboration, but these possibilities are not always obvious. Like any tool, mastery comes from study and practice. What this means looks different for everyone, whether curating an online brand and feed, creating new digital sounds, or building a website. These practices are empowering, simultaneously helping us learn skills and contemplate where we want to explore in this digital age.

The tools and instruments we use are our mediums, and they shape the messages we create. Our instruments can be a guitar and amplifier, voice and microphone, or a computer and the internet. Regardless of configuration, we have to study our medium if we want to control our message. Over time, our mediums will change, but there are foundations that remain, from rhythm, melody, and harmony, to the underlying protocols of software and computer networking. Understanding these foundational elements help us adapt to new instruments as the technologies change around us.

It can also be helpful to think about our position as users of digital technology. "If you're not the customer, you're the product" is an adage often associated with the advertisement-based business model of social media. In fact, this phrase was written about another mass medium that sold our attention to advertisers. It's from a 1973 short art film titled, *Television Delivers People*.

With social media, the medium has evolved, but the foundation for this model remains. This system of connecting and advertising is part of our digital world. With it, we can feel somewhat trapped, whether we're staring at our smartphone instead of engaging with other people, or obsessively checking the news and social media. But as we reflect on this system we can make more informed, authentic decisions about how we use technology.

The search for metaphysical truth and understanding reverberates across generations of philosophers, musicians, and entrepreneurs: from the Vedas, Pythagoras, and Boethius, to Bernstein and Tesla, who apocryphally said, "If you want to find the secrets of the universe, think in terms of energy, frequency and vibration." In this context, music can be our brain waves and cells in our bodies, the tectonic plates shifting, the planetary movements in the solar system.

We may never fully understand the rich harmonies of our bodies, our instruments, and worlds around us, but that's exciting. This is why we love music, because no matter how skilled we are, there is always more to learn. For many of us, it's this process of discovery that brings joy. When Tesla speaks of energy, frequency, and vibration, I think of music. It's a through line in philosophy, science, technology, culture, and, most importantly, our own lives. Nothing is created or destroyed, only transferred through context and time.

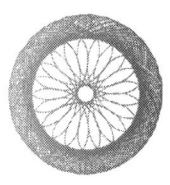

Rʜʏᴛʜᴍ, ʜᴀʀᴍᴏɴʏ, ᴍᴇʟᴏᴅʏ: I ᴄᴏɴsɪᴅᴇʀ ᴛʜᴇsᴇ ᴛʜɪɴɢs ᴀᴄʀᴏss ᴍʏ ʟɪғᴇ. Patterns, call and response, consonance and dissonance: I work with these each day in my teaching, research, and personal relationships. Music is not just organized sound. It's a philosophy that humans have always studied, molded and worked with.

Music can be anything we want it to be, even if it doesn't seem like music to others. To me, music means learning, sharing and growing. It's working to be in harmony and rhythm with ourselves and those around us. We learn about the music that surrounds us; the music that's embedded into our lives, our favorite artists and songs, our favorite instruments and software. Our favorite musicians become heroes and their sounds become myth and legend. We intuitively begin to learn about the history and cultural context that surrounds something we so cherish.

When I think of my favourite musicians, I see my heroes and teachers — Charlie Parker, Miles Davis, Valerie, and Steven — all in one group. Though their activities and impact are all different, they have all shaped my life. They taught me collectively about improvisation, challenging norms, holistic success, making and redefining art, playing, performing, and reflecting. They taught me about music. I can use pieces of them in my life, and hope I can make my students feel similarly inspired to how I felt around these mentors.

In an essay titled *Teachers and Pupils*, Albert Einstein wrote: "The principal art of the teacher is to awaken the joy in creation and knowledge...the wonderful things you learn in your schools are the work of many generations, produced by enthusiastic effort and infinite labour in every country of the world. All this is put into your hands as your inheritance in order that you may receive it, honour it, add to it, and one day faithfully hand it on to your children."

These words represent my ideals and aspirations as a teacher, and I've been inspired by them for over a decade. I even wrote this quote in my high school yearbook as a final graduation message. At the time, it was mostly a passive-aggressive jab at teachers who I felt didn't respect my creativity or individuality. What I didn't realize was the significance this phrase would play across my entire life.

As a teacher, I try to help my students think in new ways. They are going through life transitions and transformations, and I try to focus on what they need as individuals. The classroom is not a space for me to fill students' heads with knowledge. Today the internet, books, friends and fellow classmates are all excellent sources of knowledge. Students must construct their own conception of a topic, and my role is more of a guide, mentor, and facilitator. I can add context, help to find relationships between topics, and shape the subject matter to be valuable for their individual journeys. I want my students to learn something about a topic, but more importantly, I hope they can learn something about themselves.

Chapter 11: Musical Thinking

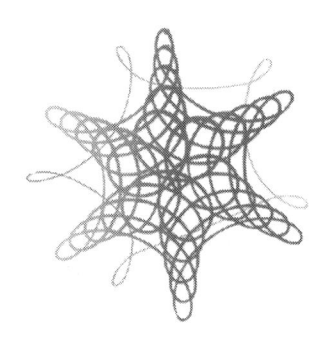

WE MAY UNDERSTANDABLY LOOK AT SUCCESS, WEALTH, AND HAPPINESS AS GOALS TO BE ACHIEVED, AS "MAKING IT", BUT WE WILL LIKELY NEVER FEEL LIKE WE'VE MADE IT. There will always be a new goal, a new challenge, a new form of making it. We are always working and reflecting to shape our lives, moving through states of pushing and flowing — a simplistic spectrum for exploring the movement and balance of powerful forces.

You may have heard of the "flow state", a popular concept for explaining those moments when we feel in the zone. We've all experienced this feeling, maybe writing, when a new idea seems to just flow out of us, or performing, when we've mastered a groove, when we're in the pocket, flowing over a beat, playing intuitively with those around us. Psychologist Mihály Csíkszentmihályi first coined the term in the 1970s, referencing the feeling of being carried along in a water current.

"Pushing" can often be thought of as the work that gets us into this flow state. It takes struggle, energy, and difficulty. We know what we want but we're not quite sure how to get there, and we're experimenting with all sorts of ideas. There is no flowing without pushing and vice versa.

Pushing introduces dissonance into our lives, which often feels disharmonious. We may be uncomfortable, stressed or nervous, because we're working towards something new and unfamiliar. It can be difficult, but over time, and with effort, our pushing becomes flowing. We feel more confident, more natural, and the dissonance resolves.

We've touched briefly on some of the greatest improvisers and composers of all time: Charlie Parker and Johann Sebastian Bach. Today they are remembered as geniuses, their transcendent improvisations and compositions continue to resonate with humans long passed their deaths. Yet their lives were dominated by pushing. Bach made his living by tutoring students and playing for the church. Parker famously spent 14 hour days in a backyard woodshed practicing saxophone. By pushing themselves to these lengths, both musicians achieved profoundly deep flow, but they pushed hard to get there.

We can also change our pushing and flowing contexts. Pushing can feel good, it feels productive, like we're working towards something. It can be easy to push, especially for something we're passionate about, like learning a song, applying for a new job, or advocating for ourselves. In these situations, flowing can be extremely difficult, even though it might be more important. Sometimes, we need to let the current carry us along. We can't always push, especially when we're dealing with things outside of our control. We can't push people into doing what we want, or push time to move on our preferred schedule. I couldn't push to become a successful professional guitarist. Sometimes flowing is more productive, and its own struggle. But this patience can reap the greatest rewards.

Pushing and flowing is a helpful spectrum for reflecting on personal progress. We are forced to push when we're in school, as we learn new concepts. In my experience, the happiest people continue to push outside of school, challenging themselves and growing. I see people pushing to enter the flow state and finding great success, but then pushing out of their comfort zone again to find new success and happiness.

With pushing and flowing, it's not and/or, it's both/and, we're always doing both, It's never one or the other, we're pushing and flowing across contexts, dimensions, and relationships.

We learn early in our lives that pursuing dreams does not mean having fun all the time. It means balancing fun with struggle. We know this feeling first hand, whether from learning to read, practicing our instruments, playing sports or doing any other activity. Getting better at something is frustrating. Some things come easier than others, but nothing comes easy.

Shaping a life in music is an endless process and our experiences can be exciting, inspiring, overwhelming, frustrating, and tiring. We must do things that scare us, push forward and pursue what is hard in order to feel that we tried our best.

Personal struggle often ensures we are pursuing our passions. Happiness is less about the goal, and more about the direction, the combinations, and connections. We push, flow, and pivot, developing an interconnected set of skills, relationships and experiences that can help us feel authentically successful. What this exactly means can be unclear, because authenticity is an elusive and intangible quality. It involves doing the things we love and pursuing what makes us happy — it's about our beliefs, our values, and what we think is important. We must nurture our passions while exploring how to offer value to the wider world.

This is a process of growth and it takes time and struggle; it's about making something new and more. It requires teaching and learning, composing and curating, performing and improvising. We synthesize our knowledge and skills, while contemplating and challenging our personal and cultural assumptions:

How do we think musically?

How does music shape experience, memory, and cognition?

What does music teach?

These questions have no single answers, but are worth asking. They're not empirical, they can't be quantified or universally measured. They're intuitive and personal.

We've looked at what it means to shape a life in music and live musically. A life in music is an external process — it's about engaging with the community, the industry, and finding a place. Living musically is internal, it's soulful, and only we know how it affects and fulfills us. These concepts are separate but connected.

Everyone's conception of music is different. But we all begin from a united foundation — a love of music and the imperative to create and share. While our relationship with music involves sound, we inherently know it's much more.

Music influences and is influenced by the people, location, instruments, and technologies used to create and share, as well as the cultural, technological, political and economic environments around it. It's a system of belief and a tool for understanding the universe. Music is not a singular, but a representation of humanity in a given moment.

We begin this journey by asking ourselves many of the same questions about who we are and where we want to be in the future. Working towards these answers looks different for everyone, as we curate our experiences and compose our lives. This includes personal reflection, engaging with the community and performing for a variety of audiences — being open and responsive to the moment and adapting to the situations and people around us. This is making a life in music, and it's not a one-time process. We will question, curate, and compose over and over again until we find answers that feel authentic.

Sometimes, the answers will not satisfy us, and we will feel like we have failed. These feelings are difficult to deal with, but we can remember that dissonance and conflict are necessities in life and music, and often failures become our most important lessons.

Music is interdisciplinary, regardless of configuration, instruments or style. We may think of rhythm, melody, and harmony. These expand to ear training, sight reading, improvisation, performance, and recording. Then further to the industry itself, our current technology, political and economic climates, philosophy, and culture. These elements all interact on multiple levels and are part of a complex system.

Music isn't made in a vacuum, but this is true of all endeavors, commercial, technological, social. We need to embrace the developments of the information age while being cognisant of centuries-old musical traditions: composition, songwriting, improvisation, stagecraft and beyond. How do they relate to each other? How do they transfer to what you're doing now, and what you want to do in the future? By surveying these considerations and reflecting on your passions, you can be cognisant and self-directed in choosing what you pursue and what skills to further develop.

A life in music is an effort to find balance. Balance between pushing and flowing, dissonance and consonance, tension and release, dreams and realities, goals and skills. This is only a glimpse into these concepts and questions that we'll confront on multiple occasions, in different environments, with different people, using different tools, having different amounts of money, and feeling different levels of happiness. These questions won't ever truly resolve, and that's ok. But by asking these unanswerable questions, we're living musically.

Chapter 12: Emergence

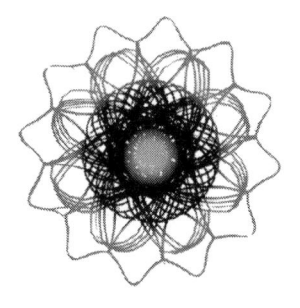

People ask me if I still make music. The answer is "yes", but my explanation isn't what they're expecting. Most people have the idea that "making music" is recording or playing on stage, which I haven't really done in years. Making music means having an impact on the communities around me. I am practicing and performing, shaping my narrative, searching for authenticity, mentoring and learning, and most importantly, engaging with culture and technology. There are no straight paths to finding "success" in music, but there are ways to open yourself to new opportunity and growth.

An important starting point is realizing that the question can't be: Do you want to make it in the music industry, or make it as a musician? Rather, it's: Do you want to live musically? And if the answer is yes, then go from there. This existential question manifests itself in everyday decisions — when you choose to pick up your instrument, introduce yourself to new people, read about your favourite artists, or do anything else on the infinite plane of musical activities. These seemingly small actions combine to propel you forward towards your goals.

But what are your goals? What does it mean to live musically? What should you do? Beginning to answer this can be difficult, and reframing the questions can help. Instead of "what should you do?", the question becomes:

Where are you?

Where do you want to go?

Where can music take you?

With these questions, you begin to see a path. You have a goal in the distance, and now you need to try to move towards it. As you learn new things, gain more experiences, and develop new relationships, you must ask yourself these questions over and over again, because the goal will change. This is the journey of living musically. You can start from anywhere, you already have, it's up to you to keep moving.

On this journey it's possible that you will encounter failure. In fact, it's guaranteed. If you're able to fail and move forward, you'll learn that it is strengthening. For me, it was failing as a guitarist. This was life altering and inherently dramatic because my singular focus had been hindering my broader view of self. Once I accepted that I wasn't going to be a successful professional guitarist, I opened up to a lot more opportunities and possibilities, and importantly, found joy in the guitar once again. I learned that all experiences are valuable, we are not our past failures or successes, but they are part of us.

At some point, you are going to quit. You are going to try again. You are going to try different things, some which at first may not feel truly like "music." The more you expand your definition of music, the more you will increase your chances of success. By trapping yourself in one conception of what music is and how to be successful, you're limiting yourself. You can allow music to be anything, as long as it feels authentic. The unhappiest people are the ones who consistently do things that are inauthentic to themselves. The struggle of every young musician is to find their voice and sound, whether it's on stage, in the classroom, boardroom, or anywhere else.

Part of the way we choose what to study and pursue is by following the narrative we would like to have, we follow our dreams. We can't pick all of our conditions but we can try to make decisions that leverage our passions and strengths. Our future lives and careers might not look like our current ideal scenarios, our futures might not look like our dreams. Therefore we must follow our dreams and simultaneously account for the new and the unexpected. We must be ready to remix and reformat in order to place ourselves in the best contexts for success.

This perspective has helped me. I've come to understand that there are no clear answers and that's what's exciting, that's where the opportunities lie. To balance our passion for music, our own desires, and the needs of the community. We must work to find our own unique sound and authentic voice. We need to work with and around music and do the things that scare us most, all the while staying true to that most fundamental human imperative to create sounds and experiences to share.

Music is always changing as an art, product, and industry. Flux is the status quo. Though we cannot know where it's going next, we can prepare for it by studying the past, immersing ourselves in the present and embracing the future, even if it feels scary or unfamiliar. We can do this in a variety of ways, including school, volunteering and work experience. Mentorship has been an important aspect of learning in my life. My musical heroes served as gateways into history and inspirations for my own journey. My teachers and personal mentors gave me role models who have shifted with this changing industry and an understanding of music in its multiple forms, reshaping the perspective of what I could do in my own life. Yet one mentor, school class or book will never be enough. You must be active, self-directed, taking these stories, experiences, and pieces of advice, and recontextualizing them for your own journey.

When we look within, we may see a vast, diverse and unconnected set of skills and interests. Yet with time, perseverance and work, these interests can be aligned and developed. Our lives can seem somewhat random, but by reflecting on our experiences — whether they are positive, sad, boring, or difficult — we're able to articulate lessons and put them into action. Our goals naturally change over time, but we all need to start somewhere. We can look to our peers, mentors, or people we idolize for ideas of how to move forward, but they can't tell us what a good situation is for ourselves, or when to try a new direction. They can't tell us when we're failing or succeeding. Nobody knows these things better than ourselves.

We try to create our own path and in doing this we realize that there is no success without risk and we can't avoid difficult decisions. It's important that we step up and face these decisions head on because it's through this process that we shape ourselves into the people we need to be. We all have to figure out what is important to us and what we value. We will have a lot of information thrown at us, and we need to turn it into inspiration and context, a path forward. Our paths are personal, there is no "right", there is only how we feel and what we do. We need to chase our dreams, but we can't be too focused on any specific path. We need to be open to learning, reflecting, and adapting.

Across space, time, and technology, infinite strands of musical meaning weave together to form the rhythms, harmonies, and melodies of life. From manuscript to mobile device, from symphony orchestra to streaming service, from guitar to outboard gear, this perspective imbues all music with rich legacies of innovation. There are many ways to understand these progressions and the waves of political, economic, and cultural influence around them. We can't definitively know them all, but studying these facets help us find ourselves and our own spaces.

We are the sum of our parts, but from that sum can emerge something greater, we can create something unique and unprecedented. We know it's possible because this principle manifests in our love for music, the musical imperative. There is joy in creation but also conflict; we struggle to balance opposing forces and resolve dissonance into consonance. There is no singular "music", "success", or "context" — we have to decide for ourselves.

Bibliography

Albert Einstein. (1949). Teachers and Pupils in *The World As I See It*. Philosophical Library.

Marc Andreessen. (2011). *Why Software Is Eating the World*. Andreessen Horowitz.

Aristotle. Book 8 in Politics, Written 350 B.C.E, Translated by Benjamin Jowett. (1994-2009). The Internet Classics Archive.

Arthur 'Big Boy' Crudup. (March, 1947). *That's All Right*. RCA Victor.

Astra Taylor. (2008). Cornel West in *Examined Life*. Zeitgeist Films.

Berlin Philharmonic & Rafael Kubelik. (1963). *Handel: Water Music / Music for the Royal Fireworks*. Deutsche Grammophon.

Blank Banshee. (September 1, 2012). Teen Pregnancy on *Blank Banshee 0*. Bandcamp.

Charlie Parker. (2002). *The Complete Savoy & Dial Master Takes*, recorded between 1945 and 1948. Savoy Jazz Records.

Cornel West. (1999). Part Seven - The Arts in *The Cornel West Reader*. Basic Civitas Books.

Cupcakke. (December 30, 2016). *Cupcakke - LGBT*. YouTube.

David Byrne. (2012). *How Music Works*. McSweeney's Publishing.

Diana Ross. (September 13, 1984). It's Your Move on *Swept Away*. RCA Records.

Donald Grout, Peter Burkholder, & Claude Palisca. (2006). *A History of Western Music*. W.W. Norton.

Donald Passman. (2003). All You Need to Know About the Music Business. Free Press.

Elvis Presley. (July 5, 1954). *That's All Right*. Sun Records.

Geoff Wonfor & Bob Smeaton. (1995). *The Beatles Anthology*. Apple Corps Limited.

Grandmaster Flash and the Furious Five. (July 1, 1982). *The Message*. Sugar Hill Records.

Joe Liggins and his Honeydrippers. (April 20, 1945). *The Honeydripper (Parts 1 and 2)*. Exclusive Records.

John Bransford, Ann Brown, & Rodney Cocking. (1999). *How People Learn: Brain, Mind, Experience, and School*. National Academy Press.

John Mayer. (September 12, 2006) *Continuum*. Columbia Records.

John Miller. (2007). *The Holistic Curriculum*. University of Toronto Press.

Karl Marx & Frederick Engels. (2010). Productivity Of Capital, Productive And Unproductive Labour in *Marx & Engels Collected Works Vol 34: Marx: 1861-1864*. Lawrence & Wishart. Internet Archive.

Ken Burns & Geoffrey Ward. (2000). *Jazz: A Film by Ken Burns*. PBS.

Lawrence Lessig. (2008). Remix: Making Art and Commerce Thrive in the Hybrid Economy. Internet Archive.

Led Zeppelin. (October, 1969). Whole Lotta Love on *Led Zeppelin II*. Atlantic Records.

Leonard Bernstein & New York Philharmonic Orchestra. (1990). The Unanswered Question on *Charles Ives: Symphony No.2*. Deutsche Grammophon.

Leonard Bernstein & Stephen Sondheim. (1957). *West Side Story (Original Broadway Cast)*. Columbia Records.

Leonard Bernstein. (1966). *The Infinite Variety of Music*. Simon and Schuster.

Leonard Bernstein. (1976). *The Unanswered Question: Six Talks at Harvard*. Harvard University Press.

Lesley Mahoney. (October 24, 2008). *John Mayer: Converting Information to Inspiration*. Berklee College of Music News.

Lucien Hughes. (February 29, 2016). *SUNDAY SCHOOL*. Youtube.

Macintosh Plus. (December 11, 2011). *Floral Shoppe*. Bandcamp.

Margaret Cheney. (1981). *Tesla, Man Out of Time*. Prentice-Hall.

Mark Katz. (2004). *Capturing Sound: How Technology Has Changed Music*. University of California Press.

Marshall McLuhan. (1964). *Understanding Media*. McGraw-Hill.

Mihaly Csikszentmihalyi. (2008). *Flow: The Psychology of Optimal Experience*. Harper Perennial.

Miles Davis & Quincy Troupe. (1989). *Miles, the Autobiography*. Simon and Schuster.

Miles Davis. (August 17, 1959). *Kind of Blue*. Columbia Records.

Miles Davis. (March 30, 1970). *Bitches Brew*. Columbia Records.

Miles Davis. (June 30, 1992). *Doo-Bop*. Warner Records Inc.

Muddy Waters. (1963). *You Need Love*. Chess Records.

Nityananda Misra. (July 25, 2018). *The Om Mala: Meanings of the Mystic Sound*. Bloomsbury Publishing.

Noam Chomsky. (2002). Media Control: The Spectacular Achievements of Propaganda. Seven Stories Press.

O Gosvami. (1957). The Story of Indian Music: Its Growth and Synthesis. Asia Publishing House.

Piet Stryckers, René Van Laken, Marcel Ketels, Job Boswinkel, Jan Van Elsacker & Guillemette Laurens. (1996). Adieu mes amours By Josquin Des Prez on *Vous ou la mort (Flemish Courtly Love Songs)*. Cantus Records.

Rae Sremmurd. (September 22, 2016). Rae Sremmurd - Black Beatles ft. Gucci Mane (Official Video). YouTube.

Richard Dawkins. (1989). *The Selfish Gene*. Oxford University Press.

Richard Serra & Carlota Schoolman. (1973). *Television Delivers People.*

Shuggie Otis. (October 1974). *Inspiration Information*. Epic Records.

Steve Jobs. *iPod Introduction*. (October 23, 2001). allaboutSteveJobs.com.

The Beatles. (1966). *Revolver*. Calderstone Productions.

The Notorious B.I.G.. (September 13, 1994). *Ready to Die*. Bad Boy Records.

Wayne Shorter. (June 1966). *Speak No Evil*. Blue Note Records.

William Gibson. (2012). Dead Man Sings in *Distrust That Particular Flavor*. G.P. Putnam's Sons.

Wolfenstein OS X. (September 11, 2015). *Vaporwave - A Brief History (Documentary)*. Internet Archive.

Young Thug. (January 16, 2017). *Young Thug - Wyclef Jean [Official Video]*. YouTube.

ABOUT THE AUTHOR

Noah Schwartz's journey through music, media and design is typical of creative careers in the 21st century. As a young guitarist at Berklee College of Music, he experienced music's digital upheaval, and witnessed how musicians with a singular focus struggled while multifaceted creators and entrepreneurs thrived. From there, Schwartz worked on many sides of the industry — including with artists and bands, record labels and music technology companies.

Today, he's a professor of music and digital media, translating his experiences and lessons learned for university students and working with the next generation of musicians and creative professionals.

Schwartz holds a Bachelor's Degree in Professional Music from Berklee College of Music, a Master's in Media Production from Ryerson University, and is currently a PhD candidate at the Ontario Institute for Studies in Education at the University of Toronto.

Manufactured by Amazon.ca
Bolton, ON